HOOKING IN

The Underground Computer Bulletin Board
Workbook and Guide
1984 Edition

by
Tom Beeston
and
Tom Tucker

Edited by

Ellis Kadison

Published by ComputerFood Press, Division of Coltrane and Beach

31754 Foxfield Drive, Westlake Village, CA 91361

IMPORTANT

Due to the dynamic nature of the computer industry, neither the publisher nor the authors assume any responsibility or liability for loss or damages caused or alleged to be caused, directly or indirectly, by applying any information regarding software or hardware described in this book. This includes, but is not limited to: any loss of business, anticipated profits or damages resulting from the use of information or alterations herein contained. Further, the publisher and authors assume no responsibility for errors or omissions. The sole judge of his or her skills or abilities in using the information contained in this book is the reader.

TOM BEESTON, TOM TUCKER

HOOKING IN

— The Underground Computer Bulletin Board Workbook and Guide 1984

Copyright © 1983 by ComputerFood Press, Div. of Coltrane and Beach
ISBN 0-913425-00-1

Coltrane and Beach
31754 Foxfield Drive
Westlake Village, CA 91361
P.O. Box 6249
Thousand Oaks, CA 91359

Distributed by Kampmann and Company — 9 E. 40th St. New York, N.Y. 10016
(212) 685-2928

PROLOGUE

Underground Bulletin Board Systems . . . the newest, most intriguing source of just about every kind of information, dialogue, and service imaginable. And if it hasn't been initiated yet, have no fear, it will be. Maybe even by you!

For those of you who haven't been there before, in this book, we give you all the information you need to enter and explore this new world. Including a BLITZ COURSE IN TELECOMPUTING, BUYERS' GUIDE TO MODEMS — (Don't worry! If you don't know what a modem is, a few pages ahead, and you'll be up there with the experts.) — and a step-by-step guide to getting started, including sample menus and procedures.

For those of you who have, we've provided some useful tools and procedures that will make this whole business of telecomputing even more enjoyable. As well as some interesting side trips into its history, some tips from system operators, and a few points of etiquette which will make you a welcome communicator wherever you may wander.

Just as importantly, however, this workbook and guide contains an ON-LINE LOGBOOK, an ELECTRONIC MAIL ADDRESS BOOK, and a DIRECTORY containing over 400 verified (as of October, 1983) telephone numbers you can call up on your computer. Further, the DIRECTORY is formatted in workbook fashion, so that you may take notes and keep a journal about your experiences on-line.

In keeping with this workbook concept, every so often you will find a lined "Notes" page. Please make use of these. From our experience, we have found this makes "Hooking In" even more personal.

You will also find ways, means and places for acquiring free Public Domain software, and suggestions for starting your own system for either business or pleasure and/or a combination of both.

And all of the above are only a portion of the many features to be found within these covers. We suggest, therefore, that the first thing you do is read through the Table of Contents, thumb through the sections themselves, and then get down to the real business of either learning how to telecompute, or, in the event that you already know that, learning how to do it better.

When the man said, "Come one, come all, there's something for *everybody*!", he must've known telecomputing was on its way!

So Participate . . . Hook In! . . . Enjoy!

TABLE OF CONTENTS

──────────── SECTION I ────────────

THE UNDERGROUND

─────────────── SECTION II ───────────────

FROM THE PUBLIC DOMAIN

─────────────── SECTION III ───────────────

ROADMAPS

SECTION IV

DIRECTORIES

CHAPTER IX

* Computer Bulletin Board Numbers
Sorted By Area Code And Number

* Bulletin Board Numbers In A Workbook Format
For Recording Changes And Additions

SECTION V

ON-LINE LOGBOOKS

CHAPTER X

* Personal Equipment Log * BBS On-Line Logbook

CHAPTER XI

SECTION VI

RESOURCES

This book is dedicated to the spirit of Norman Sholin.
He would have enjoyed "Workin' the Boards."

Acknowledgements:

   The authors would like to thank the following people without whose moral support and efforts, this book would not exist – Margot Beeston, Nancy Jacobs, Darryl Henderson and Magdelyn Hayes of SOS Computers (L.A.), Ellis Kadison, Stephen Poe, Dennis & Sev Coon, Angel Tompkins, Laurel Tucker, Kim Levitt, and Barry Coe.

Layout Design – MARK HELIGER
Cover Design – ELLIS KADISON & MARK HELIGER
Cover Illustration – TOM LUCAS
Illustrations – LEOPOLD DURANONA

This book was word-processed on a KAYPRO II, and set in Frutiger and Optima, via electronic interfacing, by COMMTYPE of Los Angeles, (213) 938-TYPE.

Printed in the U.S.A. by Delta Lithograph Co., Van Nuys, (213) 781-2460.

SECTION ONE

THE UNDERGROUND

CHAPTER I

* THE UNDERGROUND – WHAT'S ALL THE EXCITEMENT ABOUT?

* The Computer Revolution Is Going Public * Hooking In
* What Is The Underground? * What Is A Bulletin Board Anyway?
* The Two Basic Types of Bulletin Boards * Who Runs
Bulletin Boards? * The Future?

THE COMPUTER REVOLUTION IS GOING PUBLIC

Just think! — the computer you bought to balance your checkbook, adjust your recipes, save the galaxy from alien hoards (in your spare time, of course), or just to get the kids off your back (or your parents out of your room) — that same computer can easily be made to do something that boggles the mind . . . go ON-LINE! To be on-line is to communicate with other computers anywhere in the world.

The potential for true global communications is here today. The world is experiencing a revolution that is tying home computers, telephones, television sets, and communication satellites into a vast interactive network. And this book will help you join in. (Or, if you already are one of the many in the forefront of the movement, provide you with some useful information and tools, so that you may enjoy it even more.)

A large number of people are now using their personal computers to talk to other computers over the telephone lines (telecomputing; see Chapter II). For many home users, this is the most exciting and rewarding aspect of the entire computer revolution.

HOOKING IN

Connecting your computer into the telephone lines opens the door to an awesome universe that was once reserved for government, big business, and the academic community. For years these groups have been retrieving various types of information from huge central computers. Now all this information is available to you.

These information banks are called databases. Using these databases requires time and money. Thousands of people are using these services daily.

But this book is concerned with still another dimension. What we are talking about is the twilight zone, the wild west of home computing where ANYTHING can happen. The door is wide open to *any*one with *any* computer that is connected to *any* telephone.

WHAT IS THE UNDERGROUND?

The "Underground" is a loosely formed network of computer bulletin board systems created for the most part by home personal computer users. "Underground" as applied to the computer network is used synonymously with "little known". A computer bulletin board provides a means for interactive mass communication on an individual basis. Simply put, individuals, by means of "underground" bulletin boards, communicate all sorts of information to other individuals who hook in.

It is this *interactive* quality that differentiates a computer bulletin board from television, newspapers, radio, films and all other mass media which essentially transmit information in one direction.

WHAT IS A BULLETIN BOARD ANYWAY?

In this book the terms "bulletin board", "bulletin board system", "BBS" and "boards" are all used interchangeably.

Strictly speaking, a bulletin board is a special program that allows a computer to operate as a message system. If you make the decision to hook in, you can call (at your convenience) any of hundreds of computer bulletin boards, establish contact, and exchange information on just about any subject. You can leave messages of any type you wish or comment on any message that interests you.

Perhaps because of pre-conceived visuals, "bulletin board" is not the best name for this new phenomenon. But it *is* the one most commonly used. Whereas the old fashioned supermarket type bulletin board (with which everyone is familiar) is only a one-way communication, the computerized version is at the very least two-way. (Once again, the key: *interacting*!)

Most underground bulletin boards are free. The only charge for using these systems (with a few exceptions) is the cost of the phone call itself. And if you call during the low-rate hours, this can be pennies.

THE TWO TYPES OF BULLETIN BOARDS

Though there are multitudinous varieties of bulletin boards, essentially they all fall into one of two general categories:

- Single Purpose Message Boards
- Message and File Transfer Boards.

Single Purpose Message Boards

The simplest type of BBS is a single purpose message board. Here callers leave messages to be read by any other person who calls in. Private messages can be addressed to a specific individual. Messages of this sort are referred to as 'Electronic Mail'. (See Chapter IX). You can call into these bulletin boards no matter what type of computer you own.

Message And File Transfer Boards

A more sophisticated type of bulletin board is one that acts not only as a simple public message board, but also has the ability to transfer programs or files between the two computers. With the proper communications program and a means of storage (cassette or disk), your computer can receive and store programs and files from another computer. This is called *down* loading. This process also takes place in reverse. Programs or files of useful information *you* have created can be sent from your computer to the system you are calling. Obviously, this is called *up*loading. When you upload, other interested callers can then benefit from your efforts and resources.

Just being able to download a program does not guarantee that you will be able to run it. Some programs are designed specifically for certain computers. For example a program for the APPLE II might well take a certain amount of modification to run on an Atari or a VIC-20.

The more expertise you develop, the simpler up and down loading becomes. Of course there will be those who have neither the experience – (All it takes is practice!) – nor the desire to delve this deeply into it. For these, there are still plenty of other available activities – probably just as informative and (for them, certainly) more fun. After all, who says you have to be able to tune a Ferrari in order to enjoy a Sunday drive to the beach?

WHO RUNS BULLETIN BOARDS?

Some bulletin boards are run by progressive businesses to promote and receive feedback on their products. You'll find companies that are already taking orders through bulletin boards they have set up.

The most exciting and diverse boards, however, are run by individuals who are home computer user/enthusiasts. These people are called sysops – short for SYS(tem) OP(erators). Sysops dedicate a computer to running a bulletin board. They operate these boards according to their own personalities and interests. Sysops need not be present for the bulletin board to work. If the sysop is there when someone calls in, he/she can participate in a "real-time" live conversation with the caller. Sysops can also interact with their callers by posting public messages or leaving electronic mail.

Local user groups (computer clubs) also run and maintain boards. The members of these groups pool their time and resources to do so.

THE FUTURE?

The full impact of the computer revolution is yet to be realized. Now is your chance to help shape tomorrow. Some highly likely developments are:

- Mass dissemination of any and all types of information
- Decentralization of the work force (cottage industries)
- Special interest items made instantly available to a widely scattered audience.

For more specific examples check Chapters III and V.

(11)

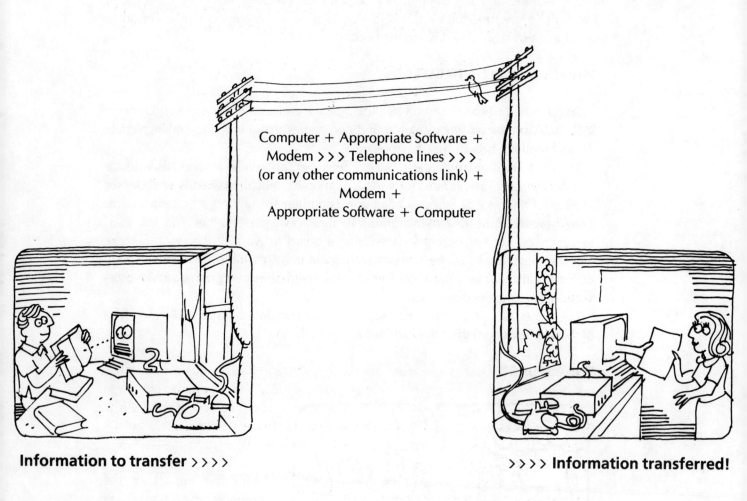

Computer + Appropriate Software +
Modem > > > Telephone lines > > >
(or any other communications link) +
Modem +
Appropriate Software + Computer

Information to transfer > > > >

> > > > **Information transferred!**

CHAPTER II

* * A *BLITZ* COURSE IN TELECOMPUTING * *

* What Is Telecommunications ? * What Is Telecomputing?
* What Do You Need To Telecompute?
(Computer-Appropriate Software – Telephone – Modem)
* Why Do They Call It A Modem ? * Common Terms Associated With
Modems * What To Look For When Buying A Modem

. . . A *BLITZ* COURSE IN TELECOMPUTING . . .

. . . IN 25 WORDS OR LESS . . .

Information to transfer > > > >
   Computer + Appropriate Software + Modem > > > >
      Telephone lines (or any other communications link) > > > >
   Modem + Appropriate Software + Computer = **Information transferred!**

WHAT IS TELECOMMUNICATIONS ?

In the most general sense it is the transfer of any type of information from one location to another by radio, television, telephone lines, or any other means of electronic communication.

WHAT IS TELECOMPUTING?

Telecomputing is a *specific type* of telecommunications. Information is transferred from one location to another, using computers and the telephone lines. You can use your computer to "talk" to almost any other computer. Most any form of information (recipes, electronic mail, machine language routines, etc.) can be transmitted from your computer to a remote computer– be it your stockbroker's, your boss's, or your grandmother's.

WHAT DO YOU NEED TO TELECOMPUTE?

* Computer * Telephone * Modem * Appropriate Software

Any home computer can be used for telecomputing. Even the popular low-cost computers, such as the Timex/Sinclair, which sell for as low as $50 can access most of the bulletin board systems in this book. Some bulletin boards are actually running on these small computer systems.

To take full advantage of BBS's, however, the amount of available memory space is important. The more memory you have, the more you can do. Memory capacity is measured in kilobytes (K).KILO is the metric prefix for 1000. A BYTE is roughly equivalent to one character of information. 2K of memory will hold about one 8½" x 11" typewritten page (double spaced). More memory allows the use of sophisticated communications programs. Additional memory is also a must for downloading programs and sending large files. Its nice to have at least 32K, but many users have fun with a lot less.

* Appropriate Software

Software may be defined as the program which makes the hardware (computer) run. Software comes stored on disks, cassettes, cartridges, and sometimes chips. There are many excellent communication programs on the market for most brands of computers. These programs coordinate the elements of the computer system and act as "directors" of the telecommunications process.

As we said earlier, a number of public domain communications programs are available at no cost. These may be downloaded from the boards themselves. Which at first glance might seem like a Catch-22, since, understandably, in order to download these in the first place, you need the use of a communications package of some sort to begin with. However, take heart; there are legitimate, simple ways to acquire these. One of the best sources is your local users group.

If you spend much time on-line, several simple-to-use but relatively sophisticated features that are nice to have in the communications program you settle on are:

* LARGE CAPTURE BUFFER – Incoming files and programs are put into a special area of the computer's memory (buffer). The information can be saved (stored on disk or cassette) for later use.
* AUTO-DIAL – Automatically dials phone numbers that have been stored in your computer. (Some modems also have this feature built in)
* AUTO LOG-ON TO FREQUENTLY CALLED SYSTEMS – It automatically calls a bulletin board and executes the proper log on sequence. (Name, location, password, type of computer, etc.)
* ERROR CHECKING CAPABILITIES – In many cases it is desirable to transfer files as accurately as possible. Several different file transfer systems have been developed to do this. Some of these have error checking built in to compare the data received with the data sent. These transfer systems are called protocol file transfers. Protocol is simply a standard set of rules or conventions. Both computers must use the same protocol. Some communications programs will allow you to choose between several different protocols. Perhaps the most common is the Christensen protocol, used by RCP/M systems. See Chapter V for details.

* Telephone

In order for people to communicate they must establish some form of contact. The same holds true for computers. The most common link between computers today is the telephone line. (If you're really into it, you could use a radio. If you're a full-on techno-freak, there are always laser beams, fiber optics, and who knows what they've come up with in the last five minutes). If you have a telephone, either touch-tone or rotary, you have the communications link you need for telecomputing.

* Modem

A modem is simply an electronic device that allows you to hook up your computer to the telephone lines.

WHY DO THEY CALL IT A MODEM ?

Many computer words are acronyms. If you take the first letter or syllable of each word in a description of something's function, and string them together, the new term usually contains the definition within itself and offers a memory jogging device at the same time. So, armed with that knowledge and a little imagination, you should be able to understand at least 25% of the computer jargon that is becoming more a part of our language each day.

MODEM, then, is an acronym. It is short for (MOD)ulator/(DEM)odulator. A modem changes the electrical impulses used by the computer into signals which can be understood and used by the phone system (modulates). It then transmits them through the phone lines to the other computer. It also receives the signals sent by the other computer's modem and converts them back into the form your computer uses (demodulates).

COMMON TERMS ASSOCIATED WITH MODEMS

AUTO-ANSWER — Modems with this feature can automatically answer the phone and establish contact with the computer that is calling. This is a must for running a BBS.

AUTO-ORIGINATE — If your computer has a clock, a modem with this feature can automatically call another computer at an appointed time, transfer files and then turn itself off. The best part is that you can be asleep!

AUTO-DIAL — This feature automatically dials your most frequently called telephone numbers. Some communication programs have this feature also.

AUTO-REDIAL — This feature can automatically redial busy numbers. It is great when you are trying to reach an extremely busy board. (Most are).

ACOUSTIC TYPE MODEM — To use this model, you simply set the phone receiver into two fitted rubber cups. Acoustic modems require no plugs or adapters. They can be used with any standard telephone. This type of modem is susceptible to high room noise. If you use an acoustic modem for long periods of time, you might want to replace the normal carbon-granule microphone in your telephone with a condenser microphone. The carbon granules have a tendency to compact after hours of modem use, which decreases the reliability of communications.

BAUD — Refers to the speed at which information is transmitted. Baud rate is roughly equivalent to words per minute. 300 baud (approximately 1 1/2 to 2 times as fast as people talk) is the most common speed found on BBS's, with 1200 baud now becoming more popular. At 1200 baud, information is transfered four times faster than at 300. Saving time saves money. See Business applications.

COMMUNICATIONS CARD — Some computers require additional hardware in order to connect a modem. (. . . but you said the PRINTER was the last thing my computer would ever need . . .)

COMPATIBILITY – There are several different modem standards. They all achieve the same end by different means. For two systems to communicate, they must use the same standard. Bell 103 (300 baud) is the most common.

Others include Bell 212A and Racal-Vadic (1200 baud). Some modems offer a choice of standards.

DIRECT CONNECT TYPE MODEM – This type of modem plugs directly into your phone jack (if your phone has a standard modular connector). Direct connect modems are not affected by room noise. Modems are either direct connect or acoustic.

DUPLEX – "Full duplex" means both sides can talk (send) and listen (receive) at the same time. We use this type of communications every day when we talk on the telephone or face to face. In "half duplex" communications, each side takes turns alternately talking then listening. Most BBS's use full duplex.

WHAT TO LOOK FOR WHEN BUYING A MODEM – If you are just getting started, a modem with the following features will allow you to access most of the numbers in this book:

* direct connect
* 300 baud
* Bell 103 compatible
* Full duplex
* F.C.C. approved.

Modems with the above features are available for around $100. See "Buyers Guide to Modems" (Section VI)

Though it is not necessary for telecomputing, a printer is a valuable addition to your system. You can use a printer to print out any incoming information you have captured in your computer. You can print the information out while you are actually on-line or later.

Printers come in two basic varieties, dot matrix and letter quality. Because of their faster speed, dot matrix printers are more suitable for telecomputing, especially if you plan to do any printing while you are on-line.

At this writing, very acceptable printers for the serious telecommunicator can be purchased for under three hundred dollars. And prices are falling daily.

With this in mind, and since printers are essentially items of personal like and dislike anyway, it is our suggestion that your best way to choose is to take a trip down to any well-stocked computer store, where you can not only see but try them.

CHAPTER III

APPLICATIONS

* What Will You Find On Computer Bulletin Boards?
* Personal Applications * Business Applications
* Ideas For Using A Computer Bulletin Board In Business

WHAT WILL YOU FIND ON COMPUTER BOARDS?

Everything from "Apple Pie Recipes" to "Which Zoo's Have Zebras", with a few X-rated subjects on the way — all this only on the most timid expeditions into this uncharted realm. By way of note, X-rated boards actually *do* exist! They usually inform you of the fact they are adult fare during sign-on. From then on the choice is yours to continue or not.

The more you get into bulletin boarding, the more you will learn that every day finds new and different specialized boards coming on line. In point of fact, many features found on the larger commercial databases are now being offered on bulletin boards — electronic shopping, advertising, special interest groups, discussions, and so forth.

Many of the messages are simply ads to buy and sell computer equipment (or anything else for that matter). Certain boards have ongoing interactive role playing games. Others specialize in free public domain software for specific makes of computers. If you can't find what you want — make it happen. Start your own board! (See Chapter VI "So You Want To Be A Sysop".)

PERSONAL APPLICATIONS (OR — WHAT'S IN IT FOR YOU?)

So many good things, it's enough to make even the most jaded cynic believe in Santa Claus. Among the many, there are boards where you can:

- Meet your mate! — Find a date!
- Download free public domain software!
- Answer questions — solve problems!
- Buy, sell, trade equipment and programs!
- Gossip about the latest products or anything else!
- Exchange, tips, ideas, gripes!
- Send and receive electronic mail!
- Play Dungeons and Dragons and other games!
- ETC. ETC. ETC.

BUSINESS APPLICATIONS

As mentioned earlier, telecomputing has already affected the business community. Multinational corporations have used computerized bulletin board systems inside of their companies for years. Now this powerful tool is easily within reach of any business, no matter how small. Today even ice cream parlors and Chinese hand laundrys are hooking in.

Some businesses run BBS's to target their products specifically to computer owners. Although at this time most of these boards are run by computer stores and manufacturers, the potential for expanding this concept into other areas is still virtually untapped.

Along this line, at least one manufacturer has set a trend worthy of consideration by other businesses in other fields. He has established a BBS specifically for customer support. The computer owner may call in at any time to read the latest updates, find answers to common questions and problems, or leave a message asking for more assistance.

Projections indicate that by 1985 one household in eight will have a personal computer. The possible exposure for cost invested could easily prove to be one of the most effective and least expensive forms of advertising available.

Incidentally, the subject of advertising on free public BBS's is an ongoing topic of debate on the boards themselves. The fate of free advertising on public boards will ultimately be decided by each individual sysop. If the sysop happens to own a business . . . .use your imagination.

A modem number listed as such in the yellow pages could put one's company on the "leading edge" of advertising and multiply its advertising dollars. You can put as much information as you like on the caller's computer screen for the price of listing one extra phone number. So it is easy to see that for the enterprising, the future is already here waiting to be put to work. Highly portable computer systems, with telecomputing abilities built in,even now are now on the market. By using these "tiny terminals", your main computer (or favorite BBS) is just a phone call away, no matter where you are.

SOME IDEAS FOR USING COMPUTER BULLETIN BOARDS IN BUSINESS

A Bulletin Board Can Be Used To:

- Distribute information to members of a company no matter where they are located. It could be accessed by employees at home, reps in the field, even secretaries in the office. Bulletin boards could make paper memos obsolete.

- Hold public (or private) conferences between departments or branches.

- Allow public access to promote and gather feedback on the company's products and services.

- Take inquiries and orders for products.

- Set up an electronic mail and message system.

As more people recognize and learn to use this technology, it almost goes without saying: bulletin boarding's commercial potential will skyrocket.

CHAPTER IV

WORKIN' THE BOARDS

* What Is Meant By "Workin' The Boards?"
* If A Human Answers Don't Panic * Suggestions For Getting
The Most Out Of This Workbook * Etiquette

What Is Meant By "Workin' The Boards"?

"Workin' the Boards" means using the underground computer bulletin board network. "Workin' The Boards" starts when:
* You sit down at your computer
* Start your communications program
* Turn on your modem
* Pick up the telephone
* Dial the number of a computer bulletin board
  (see directories)
* Wait until the other computer answers (You will
  hear the other computer's modem tone)
* Connect up your system
* Log on (give your secret password or follow
  whatever procedures the board asks for)
* Read messages, send mail, discuss problems, ideas, read ads,
meet people, play games, get programs (or contribute your own).
Do the above and you're "Workin' the Boards".

Working the boards is a singular experience. Being so new, there is nothing to compare it with.

It is the wonder of amateur radio. It is the organized chaos of C.B. It is the intrigue of espionage. It is the joy of honest communication. It is an unparalleled chance to actively help shape the future. It is here to stay.

What it becomes is up to each one of us!

The main purpose of the workbook is to provide a working environment in which to record your own personal explorations into this everchanging exciting new phenomenon.

IF A HUMAN ANSWERS, DON'T PANIC

(Honest, these conversations actually occured while verifying numbers for this book!)

. . . **ring** . . . "Hello, is this 999 999-9999?" "yes it is . . . " "I'm sorry to bother you but I'm trying to reach a computer bulletin board operator at this number. Can you help me?" "My, my, dearie, this is Worcester. I'm *sure* there are no computers here."

. . . **ring** . . . "What number are you calling please?" "111 555-1111 . . ." "What party are you trying to reach ?" "I'm trying to reach a computer bulletin

board operator at this number . . ." "I'm sorry, THAT number is the Pentagon."(SON OF "WAR GAMES" RETURNS!) "I can let you through only on official business . . ." **click** . . .

SUGGESTIONS FOR GETTING THE MOST OUT OF THIS WORKBOOK

First of all, decide which of the many different varieties of bulletin boards you would like to call. Next, look in the directory (Section IV) and pick out an appropriate number. If the BBS is a known type, review the menu and commands before logging on. This will give you an idea of what options are available to you. Keep the menu handy while you are on line.

Use the work pages (Chapter X) to keep track of: system name, address, hours, sysop's name, your password, electronic mail addresses, special interests and/or features of the board, new numbers, files downloaded, programs uploaded, messages sent and received, items for sale that interest you and so on. Write things down. A scratchpad is useful for jotting down information that you don't want to keep permanently, such as message numbers to review, etc.

Use the ON-LINE LOGBOOK (Chapter XI). Keep track of your log-on time, log-off time, and other relevant information. By referring to this record of your caller number over a period of time, you can determine the activity of a particular board. A well-kept logbook will also prove to be valuable when your phone bill arrives.

Use the ELECTRONIC MAIL ADDRESS BOOK (Chapter XII). You will make friends on-line with whom you will want to keep in contact. Write down their electronic mail addresses, the bulletin board system you find them on, and any other necessary information.

Read "SO YOU WANT TO BE A SYSOP" (Chapter VI) in order to appreciate what is involved in setting up and maintaining a BBS.

ETIQUETTE

Remember, bulletin board systems could not exist without sysops. They open up their computer homes to anyone who might drop in, and try to be the best hosts or hostesses possible. Act accordingly when you are in those homes. That way, if you want to return at some later date, you'll be accorded the warm reception due a welcome visitor.

After spending some time on a system, you may even find yourself invited in off the front porch and into one of the "backrooms". You will often discover that new areas become accessible to you when you become a regular user.

Go exploring. And remember, always treat your Sysop with the utmost courtesy. By so doing, he will keep the board open for others to enjoy.

"Takers" are people who check in, download everything they can, and then disappear. We are all takers at first. But as you become more comfortable on the boards, please contribute anything you can. Your contributions assure the very existence of these bulletin boards. So try to upload something once in a while. Even a novice can contribute something from his personal experience.

Don't hog the boards. There will be times when it is necessary to spend a long period of time on one board. Some programs can take an hour or more to download. Try to be considerate of others who want to check in and limit your time to a half hour or so per log on. Some bulletin boards have the "power" to disconnect anyone who exceeds a predetermined amount of on-line time.

Most bulletin boards have a command that allows you to sign-off. Typical of these are: BYE, OFF, and G (for Goodbye). Write down the sign-off command of the particular board you are using. If you disconnect without it, some boards fail to reset for the next caller.

SECTION TWO

FROM THE PUBLIC DOMAIN

Join the "Hook In" Generation!

CHAPTER V

SOLID GOLD (AS MINED BY DOCTOR ELECTRIC)

* Overview * RCP/M Systems – History (Continued) –
In The Beginning * Free Software * What You Need To Get It
* Log On Procedures * Types of Available Free Software
* What Kinds Of Public Domain Software Should You Get?
* Contribute * Help * Communications Programs * Christensen
Protocol and Error Checking * Your Own RCP/M Board

This chapter was contributed by the individual who writes under the name "Dr. Electric". In addition to being an acknowledged expert in many phases of computers, Dr. Electric runs his own RCP/M bulletin board.

OVERVIEW

What follows is a detailed discussion of RCP/M systems. If you are a veteran CP/M user it will present no problem. If not, don't despair. There are so many life saving programs available in the public domain that it is WELL worth your time to learn a few terms and procedures to be able to download from these systems. It's really easy!

We suggest you read this chapter once all the way through. Mark the terms you don't understand. Most unfamiliar terms are defined as they arise in the text. If not check the glossary. If it's not there, you probably won't need to know what it means to be able to download software from a RCP/M system. If it seems that you do, ask your friends, dealer or check out your local users group. At the end of this chapter several step by step log-on and download sequence are included. The hard part is deciding what you want to download.

RCP/M SYSTEMS – HISTORY

RCP/M Systems: What They Are and How They Work . . . (or "So what can I use my modem for anyway?")

RCP/M systems are the original types of bulletin boards — the ones that started it all. They provide both a model and a standard for the personal computer telecommunications network now being established. Pioneered by serious computer enthusiasts, they offer continuing help and inspiration to owners of CP/M based computer systems. RCP/M bulletin boards are true public service boards.

RCP/M stands for Remote CP/M. CP/M (Control Program/ Monitor) is currently one of the most widely used operating systems for personal computers. There are more than one million CP/M users in this country.

CP/M programs are popular because they can be run on many different brands of personal computers. There are more than three thousand commercially available CP/M programs, for almost any application. In addition to these, many programs have been written by individuals for their own specific needs and released into public domain as a public service. These programs make up a large base (over 2000 files) of free public domain software and are available to everyone.

SIG/M (Special Interest Group/Microcomputers) and CPMUG (CP/M users group) are two users groups which are set up to help catalog, collect, and distribute these programs in the most efficient manner possible. These national users groups offer Public Domain Software for little more than the cost of the disc. Check out these groups to see if they have the specific modem program your computer needs in order to download free software (more on this in a moment).

They have several catalogs containing documentation and abstracts on the various programs and files available. You can also purchase SIG/M volumes on diskettes. Write SIG/M and CPMUG for more details (addresses are in "RESOURCE" section). It is also possible to download these programs into your computer via a modem and phone line by connecting up with RCP/M bulletin board systems. This chapter will give you an idea of what types of programs are available (with recommendations) and show you how to get these programs via telecomputing.

HISTORY (CONTINUED) – IN THE BEGINNING . . .

On February 16, 1978, Ward Christensen and Randy Suess started the Chicago CBBS™ (Computerized Bulletin Board System) as a way for local computer hobbyists to leave messages for each other. Within this message system was a secret feature used in conjunction with a program Christensen wrote called "MODEM". It enabled CP/M computers calling the CBBS to send files back and forth. This file transfer capability of CBBS was initially known only by Ward and Randy and later a few others, but it was there (making this the first remote-access CP/M computer with a public message system and file transfer capabilities). Later, Christensen took the MODEM support out due to problems in keeping the system going with only 70K disks on his North Star.

The CBBS message system (written entirely in 8080 assembly language), was sold to several other computer enthusiasts, and this started several offshoots of CBBS: Keith Petersen wrote a special remote-access version of MODEM called "XMODEM", and set it up on his Royal Oak MINICBBS in the Detroit area (probably the first fully public CP/M software exchange system). Tom "C" also set up his CCCC (Calamity Cliffs Computer Club) system in Lake Forest, Illinois so that the file transfer option was public.

About the same time as the first CBBS systems were starting up, Kelly Smith's CP/M-Net™ system was up in Simi Valley, California with an XMODEM-type program called "SENDME". Dave Jaffe wrote a program called "BYE" that enabled a CP/M computer equipped with a modem to be controlled by a remote system. Howard Moulton translated an SJBBS message system written in Xitan BASIC to a more transportable version written in Microsoft BASIC called "RBBS". These people and many other experienced programmers began writing various CP/M programs and contributed them to the public domain via the bulletin boards. Thus developed what are today called RCP/M (Remote CP/M) software exchange systems.

As of October, 1983, there are over 100 RCP/M software exchange systems in the United States, and several in Canada, England and even Australia. Most of these systems are public and are available for use at no charge (or the price of a phone call if they're not local). They have LOTS of public domain software on line that you can use if you have a CP/M computer. All you need is a modem and a "MODEM" program that will allow you to access RCP/M systems and "download" the software to your computer.

FREE SOFTWARE

How good is the free software? The answer is . . . very good. Some programs are among the best around for personal computers. You will find several fantastic utilities that help make life easier for the CP/M user. There are programs to manipulate files, recover erased files, display files, and print files, as well as to scramble, spool, dis-assemble, and delete. You will also find games, graphic pictures, label printing programs, ham radio programs, enhanced operating systems, languages, and much more. Although you won't find commercially available copyrighted programs, you will find a wealth of material, some of which you can certainly adapt to your own applications. Not all programs will work on all machines, so you will have to do some experimenting.

WHAT YOU NEED TO GET IT

What's the catch to getting this free software? First of all, in order to really get anywhere, your modem program has to do more than just allow you to type text into a remote system. It needs to have a file transfer facility which will enable you to send files from the remote system to you (download), or to have the remote system receive files from you (upload). On RCP/M systems, the de-facto standard method for transferring files is via the use of a program called "XMODEM", which uses a special protocol often named for it's originator, Ward Christensen.

So, assuming you have a modem and a modem program, you're ready to connect with an RCP/M system to check out the world of public-domain software.. How do you do it? Well, to begin with, you'll need a phone number for an RCP/M system. A local one, of course, keeps the money in your pocket and not in the phone company's. You can also use the lower-cost long distance services if you want (MCI, Sprint, Western Union, etc.) A current listing of all known operating RCP/M systems can be found in the directory. Just look for RCP/M under "System Type".

LOG-ON PROCEDURES

There are many different log on procedures for the various RCP/M's. The steps I outline here may not apply for the system you call, but it should give you an idea of what to do.

You should start your modem program, and then call an RCP/M bulletin board in this book (either via an auto-dial modem or with your telephone if you are manually originating a call). Wait for it to answer and send you a carrier tone.. When you hear the carrier tone, place the phone handset in the modem (if you have an acoustic coupler type modem). If it is direct connected, just wait for a response. Once you are connected, enter terminal mode (MBOOT comes up in terminal mode by default, MODEM7 and others use a "T" command to enter terminal mode). Log on to the remote system. (You may want to enter terminal mode before you connect in order to send dial commands to your auto-dialer if you have a "smart" modem.)

On most RCP/M's, you will first have to enter a bunch of carriage returns until you get a message or question from the system. (Carriage returns are used by many RCP/M's to set the baud rate automatically to match whatever you have.) On most systems, the first question asked is "HOW MANY NULLS DO YOU NEED?". This question is mainly for hard-copy terminals which tend to lose characters at the beginning of every line during carriage return. If you are using a CRT or printing terminal with buffering, chances are you won't need any nulls, so specify 0. If you are losing characters at the beginning of every line, hang up, call the system back and ask for more nulls.

Many RCP/M's will next ask you "CAN YOUR TERMINAL DISPLAY LOWER CASE?". You should answer "Y" (YES) if lower case characters can be displayed on your system console or terminal, or "N" (NO) if you want all lower case letters converted to upper case by the RCP/M before they are transmitted to your system.

Some systems may also ask "DO YOU NEED LINEFEEDS?". If your system automatically adds linefeeds to carriage returns (TRS 80's, for example), then answer "N". Otherwise answer "Y". If you answer "Y" and everything is double spaced, remember to answer "N" next time.

After answering these first questions, you will usually see a welcome message and/or a display of bulletins (READ these – they usually have information that will help you later on). After the bulletins, you will probably be asked your first and last name and if it's your first call to the system, the city and state you are calling from. The name is used just to keep track of who's who, and can be a pseudonym if you wish, although I think proper names are preferred by most system operators (sysops). Note that some systems, such as Kelly Smith's CP/M-Net™ system, do not ask you for any log-on information at all, but simply drop you right away into CP/M.

After logging on, you will probably get a menu of functions that can be used within the message system. Most RCP/M's have a bulletin board program such as RBBS or CBBS™ which performs the log on and allows users to leave messages for each other and/or the sysop. Check th
M. On my system, for example, the "C" function will get you to CP/M, on others, "G" will do it. (Some boards use "G" for "goodbye" so carefully check the menu of the particular board you are on to make sure.) Then select this function to exit the message system and enter CP/M.

Depending on the modem program you are using, data will usually be received into memory first, and then written to disk, (most modem programs will store 16 sectors in memory before writing to disk). After the file is completely transferred, it will be closed and you will get a message to that effect. In some cases, you will be dumped back into terminal mode. In others, you will exit the modem program and will be in local mode. If you end up in local mode, be sure to re-connect using your modem program's terminal mode and disconnect from the remote system (usually by typing BYE), when you are done.

Under CP/M, you can generally use DIR (or FILEFIND or WHATSNEW or SD or some other DIR program) to see the files available on the system for downloading. (Some systems will have a HELP.COM file available on-line or a THIS-SYS.DOC file that you can TYPE for more information.) After you find a program you are interested in, you can usually use TYPE or TYPESQ to check it out to see if you really want it, and then use XMODEM to download it. (Be sure to read comments and help messages on the system you are on, as syntax can vary from one XMODEM version to another, but usually, the syntax is: "XMODEM S filename.typ", where "filename.typ" is the name of the file you wish to download.) After locating a file and starting XMODEM, you must then start your modem program to receive a file. The command is usually: "R filename.typ". If all goes well, you should see some kind of messages from your modem program as each sector is transferred across to your system.

On most RCP/M's, you log off of the system by typing "BYE" and a return as a CP/M command line. Some BBS's will also allow you to log off directly from the message system. Typing "BYE" runs a program called BYE.COM that will hang up the phone and reset the system for the next caller.

Before disconnection, on some systems, you will be asked if there are any comments. By answering "Y", you may enter comments which can only be read by the SYSOP.

If you have any problems, check to make sure that your communications interface or UART is set up for 8 bits, no parity, 1 stop bit. If you have this set-up and your modem program sends and receives data in terminal mode okay, then it SHOULD work in file transfer mode as well. Make sure you use checksum mode if your program doesn't support CRC mode. When downloading, you don't need to know which your program uses, but if you have a choice, use CRC mode. When uploading, some versions of XMODEM use R to specify receive with CRC mode, and RC for checksum mode, and others use RC for CRC mode, R for checksum mode. Type XMODEM without any option or filename and it'll probably give you a syntax help message. (More on CRC and Checksum later.)

TYPES OF AVAILABLE FREE SOFTWARE

Of the hundreds of public-domain programs out there, there are some really good ones and some really bad ones. Sifting through to find the gold isn't always easy, but it's worth it. Getting the "latest" and/or "best" version of software is difficult, especially due to the fact that several people often work on updates to the same program at the same time, and will come out with different code listing the same version number. Even so, if you ask around, you will likely find people who have one or another version that works well. You can also get help from your local user's group or RCP/M if you have problems with a particular program.

WHAT KINDS OF PUBLIC DOMAIN SOFTWARE SHOULD YOU GET?

The programs most helpful to you will depend on your particular requirements. But there are several general-purpose utilities which you will NEED and others which are really nice to have.

Two of the very first programs you should get are SQ.COM (SQ.OBJ) and USQ.COM (USQ.OBJ), written by Dick Greenlaw. These programs are written in "C" and are borrowed from the UNIX environment, but will run without modification on most standard CP/M systems. "SQ" allows you to condense (squeeze) a file in order to reduce the amount of disk space required to store it. A squeezed file also takes less time to transfer. You will also need "USQ", it's companion. USQ makes it possible to "unsqueeze" files that you download from RCP/M's, as many systems use SQ extensively to save disk space and transfer time. Two other useful companion programs are TYPESQ, which allows you to view squeezed files directly on your console without using USQ first, and PRINTSQ which will unsqueeze a file directly to the printer. Look for SQUEEZER.DOC or SQUEEZER.DQC to explain how SQ and USQ work.

A note on file types (the three characters on the end of the CP/M filename after the period):

Most XMODEMs (the program on a bulletin board which responds to your downloading commands) are set up so that you cannot transfer a file having the ".COM" extension. Therefore, sysops usually rename ".COM" files which are available for downloading to ".OBJ". When you download it, use a ".COM" extension for the filename. Generally, ".OBJ" programs are written so that they use the standard CP/M system calls and are therefore runnable as is on MOST CP/M systems. Notable exceptions include MODEM programs (CP/M has no standard system calls for modem I/O), BYE, XMODEM and other hardware-specific programs. File names with ".ASM" and ".MAC" file types are assembly language source programs. ".BAS" indicates BASIC source files, ".DOC" files are documentation, ".C" files are "C" source files, etc., etc. File types are also used as part of a file name as in "34MBRCPM.NEW". SPECIAL NOTE: IF THE MIDDLE CHARACTER OF THE FILE TYPE IS A "Q", (as in "RCPM-039.LQT"), IT USUALLY MEANS THAT THE FILE IS "SQUEEZED".

Another public-domain program which I consider to be a MUST is FINDBAD. FINDBAD allows you to check a disk (either newly formatted or a disk with files) to verify that all sectors are readable. It reads all of disk sectors, and any that it finds unreadable are locked out by being included in a "file" named "[UN-USED].BAD". I use this after formatting my disks to lock out any bad sectors, and I almost totally avoid the dreaded "BDOS ERROR ON A: BAD SECTOR" error message. CAUTION: If you run FINDBAD on a data disk it might lock out some important data if it finds a bad sector.

LU is a very useful program written by Gary Novosielski, a "library utility" used to combine related files (MODEM798.AQM, MODEM798.DQC for example) into a single ".LBR" file. The different numbers after modem (modem7, modem795, etc.) refer to different versions or revisions of the same program. LU, like SQ, is also used by sysops to save disk space/transfer time. LU will also extract files from a ".LBR" file, as will the "L" option on some versions of XMODEM if you don't want to download the whole ".LBR" file. Related LU utilities include LDIR, which will list the member files of a given library, LTYPE, which will type a selected file within a ".LBR" file, and LRUN, which will run a selected ".COM" file within a ".LBR" file.

There are MANY different directory programs out there to replace the standard built-in version that Digital Research provides for CP/M, but my personal favorite right now is SD (by David Boruff). Latest version is 4.8, I think, but I'm working on a new version with a few more goodies.

SD allows you to get a directory of your current disk and user number. It can scan all available disk and user areas automatically and also show $SYS files if desired. SD sorts the files in alphabetical order and shows the file sizes in 1K increments as well as a summary of the total disk space listed and available. Version 4.8 also has a $L option which lists the contents of any ".LBR" files encountered. The amazing thing is, it does all this with a ".COM" file of only 3K! Look for a copy of the ".DOC" or ".DQC" file for the version you find and read it for a description of all the options.

On many RCP/M's, such as my own, the sysop has eliminated the standard DIR utility so that SD (or whatever favorite DIR program the sysop likes) can be named DIR.COM. This allows people to type DIR instead of SD to get the deluxe version. Typing "DIR A: $U0ADL" on my system, for example, will show you all available files in all user areas on all disks, and will also list the contents of any library files encountered!

A few more general-purpose utilities to look for:

DU – a disk utility that lets you read and write any sector and change it any way you want.

UNERA – a handy lifesaver that can recover files you accidentally ERA'd (erased).

DIF – another utility from UNIX that compares two text files.

SSED – the companion utility to DIF, that can take the antecedent file and a ".DIF" file created by DIF to create an updated version.

CAT and NEWCAT – these useful programs allow you to keep track of where your files are on all your various disks.

RESOURCE – this program will allow you to reassemble the source for an 8080 object file.

SPELL- a "poor-man's spelling checker".

ZCPR

If your system is Z80-based, for the ultimate CP/M system, you can get ZCPR2, a public-domain replacement for the standard CP/M console command parser (CCP) written by Richard Conn. ZCPR2 gives your system a few added features over standard CP/M such as named directories (PAUL: instead of B:, for example), user-definable search path (used to allow ZCPR2 to look in more than the current disk/user area for a ".COM" file), multi-command lines, redirectable I/O and a comprehensive set of utilities that will work in concert with ZCPR2. This set of programs CAN be picked up off of RCP/M's but since there is so much of it, you might want to try and get it already installed on disk, if at all possible. It will save quite a bit of downloading time (and keep you from having a big phone bill).

One note on ZCPR2. The ideal is to get a version already set up for your particular system. If you are not very adept at assembly language systems programming, you definitely will have problems installing it. My suggestion is – try to locate someone (probably in a users group) who already has ZCPR up and running on yourparticular computer.

If you are familiar with programming and CP/M, have a copy of your system's BIOS, as ZCPR2 requires a rewrite of the cold boot routine in the BIOS in order to implement all of it's advanced features.

ZCPR version 1 is also available, without many of the advanced features. It is a lot easier to install (no BIOS changes necessary).

OTHER GOODIES

Other goodies you will want to get include:

Games – Such as CHESS, ADVENTURE, STARTREK, ALIENS, etc..

Source Files – For you programmer types.

Various ".DOC" files – You can learn a LOT by reading them.

Updated RCP/M lists – You should always get a copy of the latest listing of RCP/M systems, usually named RCPM-nnn.LQT, where "nnn" is the version number (RCPM-039.LQT is the version included below), and, yes, it's a squeezed file. If you keep up with the updates (currently updated once a month) and have SSED, you can get the ".DQF" file (a squeezed ".DIF" file), and use it to update your list. RCPMoonn.DQF, where "oo" is old version number, and "nn" is new version number, will be the file to get.
See RCPMLIST.DQC for information on how to use it with SSED to update your list.

Bulletin boards have different levels of protection, some of them are even going private. A lot of this beefed-up security is due to obnoxious pranksters who delight in screwing up systems. You should try to restrain yourself from the temptation to crash a system or you may find all your favorite free systems are no longer around one of these days . . .

CONTRIBUTE

Your participation in the RCP/M network will be more appreciated if you remember that contributions from users are the only way that RCP/M's get software to distribute, and it is hoped that most users will upload as well as download. If you find a good file on an obscure system somewhere, don't forget to pass it along to another RCP/M or two who might not have it. If you develop a new program that others might appreciate, write a ".DOC" file for it, and upload the program and documentation to an RCP/M. Public domain software is a valuable resource that we should all try to contribute to as well as benefit from.

Remember that RCP/M's are for the exchange of public domain software only. Do not upload copyrighted software for distribution on any RCP/M system.

Be sure to get a ".DOC" or ".DQC" file to go with the version you pick up and

In the same token, you shouldn't find any copyrighted software available for downloading on any RCP/M's. There are some "pirate" BBS's that do this, but I do not condone this practice, and most of the "pirates" get in trouble with one or another software company sooner or later..

HELP

Feel free to address any questions you have on particular problems to "ALL". There are many experienced users out there who can help you. The sysop can also be of assistance.

Try to read all of the bulletins, messages and ".DOC" files you can before asking questions. You might find the answer yourself.

Use TYPE to read ".DOC" files, TYPE or TYPESQ to view ".DQC" files, LTYPE to read ".DOC"/".DQC" files contained within a ".LBR" file. Many systems will respond to "HELP". (Control-C will usually exit HELP)

If you need person-to-person help on-line, you can usually use a program called "CHAT" under CP/M to talk with the sysop. Or you can use a semi-colon at the beginning of a CP/M command line to send comments to the sysop, if you know he or she is there. If you leave out the semi-colon, CP/M will look for a ".COM" file when you hit return. If the sysop doesn't respond to CHAT or your comments typed at the CP/M prompt, re-enter the message system and leave a message there for "ALL" or "SYSOP". Comments typed at the CP/M prompt or in CHAT are not saved.

Keep in mind when asking for help that sysops are usually asked for help many times a day, and cannot always answer your question right away, or may seem to ignore you.. Don't fret, just try to address the question to "ALL" or to a sysop on another system. A lot of sysops are doing it part-time and may not even check in for a couple of days. If you do your homework and ask intelligent questions, however, I think you will discover that most sysops will try to help you sooner or later.

COMMUNICATIONS PROGRAMS

Naturally, you'll want a good modem program . . . If you had to start with MBOOT, you'll need one right away so you have CRC capability and can upload as well as download. There are ninety-seven million versions of MODEM7, MODEM220, MODEM798, SMODEM, etc. out there, some of which are very machine specific and others which are very general. Most of them will require some kind of installation procedure, but if you get your first modem program working, and have the source code for it and any new version you want to install, you'll have what you need to get the new version working . . .

Be sure to get a ".DOC" or ".DQC" file to go with the version you pick up and READ it. Modem programs have different features and commands depending upon the version.

How do you get a modem program up and running on your computer?

Luckily, you don't have to re-invent the wheel. There is a special receive-only, checksum-only modem program called MBOOT that will allow you to receive a more full-fledged modem program over the phone. It's one way to start out if you can't get ahold of a friend who has a modem program for your system already set up. Look for MBOOT.DOC to describe how to get MBOOT up and running. If you have a non-standard system for which there are no modem programs available, you'll have to do a little homework to find out the proper port addresses and status register values, and modify a copy of MBOOT or a MODEM program for your system.

There are also several non-public-domain modem programs out there which also support Christensen protocol (more on this later in the chapter). However, many of the non-public versions do NOT support Christensen (XMODEM/ MODEM7) protocol. Therefore, before you buy, check the features carefully.

A few copyrighted programs which are rumored to support Christensen protocol include: SUPRTERM, (for the Kaypro II, 4 and 10); AMCALL, (for the Osborne 1); ASCOM and COMMX, (for S-100 CP/M systems and others).

CHRISTENSEN PROTOCOL AND ERROR CHECKING

The Christensen protocol is a relatively error-free way to transfer any kind of CP/M file (including ".COM" files and "squeezed" files). It can be used over standard dial-up lines (which have a lot of noise sometimes), as it has special error-detection "handshaking" built-in to insure the accurate transfer of data.

How does it work? Well, for those of you interested in the technical aspect, it basically works by dividing up the file to be sent into "sectors" (128 bytes each), sent one at a time. Each sector sent is preceded by a "start-of-header" (SOH) character and two sector number bytes and followed by a single checksum byte or two "cyclic-redundancy check" (CRC) bytes. The checksum or CRC is produced on the transmitting end and sent along with the data. On the receiving end, the checksum/CRC is computed on the received data and compared against the received checksum/CRC value. If the computed value disagrees with the received value, it indicates that a transmission error has occurred, and the receiving system will request a sector re-send with a "negative acknowledgement" (NAK). If the received and computed checksum/CRC agree, then the received sector is saved in memory or on disk and is then "acknowledged" with an "ACK" character. The receiving system will usually request re-sends only so many times (usually 10-15) for a given sector and will then "give up". This usually happens only under very noisy line conditions, or when the line becomes disconnected during a transfer operation. The checksum method is not as accurate as the CRC method, but is easier to implement, and is still hanging on as an alternative to CRC. (The CRC method used is the CCITT CRC-1v standard which is also used by other block mode protocols such as SDLC, HDLC and BISYNC. CRC's are also used on floppy disks to insure the validity of recorded data.)

YOUR OWN RCP/M BOARD

If you want to set up an RCP/M, you will need: a copy of BYE that is set up for your machine; a BBS program (CBBS™, RBBS, OXGATE, CP/M-Net™, etc.), (a BBS is optional, but either a BBS or a log on program is highly recommended); and a copy of XMODEM set up for your system. In addition you will want to poke your operating system or set up ZCPR2 in order to eliminate such commands as

ERA, REN and TYPE from the system. (TYPE will show $SYS files, and won't print out squeezed files; I use TYPE14 for TYPE.COM, which doesn't show $SYS files, but does unsqueeze squeezed files automatically.) You must be careful in setting up your system to insure at least some margin of security, or else that little brat down the street who saw War Games will call up your system and use "ERA *.*" to erase all your files!!

In addition to BYE, a BBS program and XMODEM, you should probably have CHAT, HELP and a few other ".COM" files on-line for people to use, as well as object files, source files and documentation available for downloading. Remember to try and have ".DOC" files available for all of the software (whenever possible) and watch out for uploads and/or messages filling up your system. Be prepared to answer a lot of questions from new users, as they will usually assume that you know something if you are a sysop.

RCP/M's are a real benefit to CP/M users everywhere . . . Without them, we'd all be re-inventing the wheel over and over again. Thanks to Ward Christensen and the many others who have contributed to public-domain software, we can add flexibility and power to our system without ringing up a huge bill. In fact, many public domain utilities are not available in copyrighted versions.

So put your modem to work for you. Get a modem program and join the thousands who have discovered just how useful RCP/M systems are.

"Solid gold as mined
by Dr. Electric."

"Sysops are generous
about passing tips around."

CHAPTER VI

SO . . . YOU WANT TO BE A SYSOP . . .

* Prospective Sysops - Consider The Following:
* Input From An Established Sysop * Questions To Ask Yourself
* Some Boards Are Just Boards, And Most Callers Just
Get Bored * Some Suggestions For Special Interest Boards

SYSOP – ACRONYM FOR (SYS)TEM (OP)ERATOR

Sysops perform many vital functions that are rarely appreciated. Everything they do is done out of love for the process itself. They donate their time, research, resources, advice, encouragement and even occasional disapproval, usually without fanfare or acknowledgement.

They also do the maintenance and housekeeping required to keep a computer bulletin board system operating efficiently.

Few home computers can do more than one task at a time. Since most sysops have only one computer, please realize that they are making a sacrifice when their board is online. It is a bit unsettling to see how quickly one becomes computer-dependent. The only guaranteed rewards for sysops are intangibles — inner satisfaction, useful contacts, public service and so forth.

PROSPECTIVE SYSOPS - CONSIDER THE FOLLOWING:

Input From An Established Sysop :

"Running a remote CP/M system can be a lot of fun, but it's not without headaches . . . If you have a small amount of on-line storage, you have to keep trimming the messages and uploads in order to keep the disks from filling up. There are the continuing requests for assistance that one gets from various users who're just getting started . . . You want to help, but it does get a little tiring when you have to answer the same questions over and over. I put up messages for people to read regarding the system features, but nobody ever seems to read them. They just go blundering through.

"I know it's not easy to cope with the thousand variations of RBBS and CP/M out there, but you can learn a lot if you read all the messages, notes, and .DOC files. Remember also that much of the public-domain software available works fine, but you might have to do some customizing and patching to get some of it to work on your particular hardware configuration. It's not all that difficult if you're willing to learn assembly language and/or high-level language programming. But if you'd rather not do any programming, be sure to get programs that run on ANY plain-vanilla CP/M system and you'll probably do okay . . . "

QUESTIONS TO ASK YOURSELF

1. Are your reasons for wanting your own board sound ?
   • Fortunately the answer to this is still up to the individual.

2. Is there a specific need your board can fill?
   • The possibilities are endless.

3. Do you have the time, resources and commitment needed to maintain a board?
   • For example, to delete inappropriate messages, change disks, keep board current and useful.

4. If you have only one computer, are you willing to live without it while it is being used as a BBS?

5. If you use your personal telephone number are you willing to take calls at any hour of the day or night, whether your computer is on line or not?
   • Ideally your computer should have its own telephone line. Set your modem to answer the phone quickly, preferably after one or two rings. This way your caller won't be dismayed by the prospect of disturbing people at strange hours if they misdial or if your computer is not on line.

6. Are you willing to accept the risk of abuse from inconsiderate callers?
   • Typical abuse ranges from obscene messages to wiped out disks – or even computers! The newer BBS programs make this harder to do but nothing is impossible – especially to a seasoned 12 year old computer freak. This is the twilight zone–remember?

If you can answer yes to most of these questions, do it! All you need is a personal computer, the bulletin board system program appropriate for your computer, a telephone line, and a modem that can answer your calls (See Chapter II "Blitz Course In Telecomputing").

There are many good commercial BBS programs for most brands of computers. Prices range from less than $40 to over $300, depending upon their features. There are also some excellent free (public domain) programs available from the various user groups. For more information on these programs for different types of computers, see Section VI "RESOURCES".

SOME BOARDS ARE JUST BOARDS, AND MOST CALLERS JUST GET BORED

Original RCP/M boards were set up in the spirit of public service. We hope that this spirit will continue. Ideally, system operators set the tone of their board around their own special interest – be it computers (of course), photography, gourmet cooking, amateur radio – any hobby or passion. More boards of this type are needed. If you have any imagination at all, you'll be a welcome addition to the "underground" network.

SOME SUGGESTIONS FOR SPECIAL INTEREST BOARDS

- Political Forums on any controversial issue (aren't they all!)
    Ideally every congressperson should have a board to receive feed-back from his constituents. Being on-line is a heck of a lot more fun than writing letters. A bulletin board could act as a personal "electronic poll" for collecting public opinions on any issue.

- Specialized Medical Boards
    Information and victim help groups (Cancer, Herpes, AIDS)
    Handicapped services and resources
    Prescription drug data base – side effects and compatibility
    Poison control data base – symptoms and antidotes
    Alternative Healing Arts Exchange

- Product Reviews
    Have you bought anything that you love or hate? Let the world know about it!

- Movie Reviews
    Can you believe we spent $15 to see THAT!

- Books
    Where can I find a book on . . .

- Software Evaluation
    "This is the most frustrating/wonderful documentation I've ever used."

- Gourmet's Table (The Next Byte?)
    Exchange recipes, restaurant reviews, etc. After all, what else is there besides computers and cuisine? UnlessM you're one of those who puts sex and baseball up there too.

- Alternate Energy Information Exchange
    Or, why does Arizona have the fewest solar installations in the country?

- Anonymous Psychologist (Dear Apple ?)
    To share the frustrations and solutions to life's universal problems. (You mean someone else has those feelings too? Maybe I'm NOT crazy! Then again, maybe I am!)

- Gripe Board (Rotten Apples?)

    Get it off your chest — and off your mind!

- Philosopher's Soapbox

    Expound your world view from the safety of your own den — well out of the way of stray fists.

- Lost, Found, or Stolen

    Oh where, Oh where has my new Corvette gone . . . ???

- Clearing house for bulletin board phone numbers.

    There are already several collection points online for new board telephone numbers. What is really needed is a collection point for the bad numbers! (We have over 600 to contribute). A quick cross reference of any new lists would then be a simple matter. Prospective sysops could check for a disconnected BBS number in their area and request it for their new board. This would spare new phone owners the frustration/inconvenience/irritation/ horror of late night calls directed to an ex-board. While verifying numbers, we reached a woman whose husband had terminated his bulletin board three years earlier. They are still getting calls.

NEW BOARDS

> If you are starting a new BBS, please let us know about it! We will include it in our periodic updates. Send all pertinent information: Area Code, Phone Number, Hours, System name, System type, Sysop's name — and anything else you feel is special about your board.

Send BBS info to:

ComputerFood Press
DIV. OF COLTRANE & BEACH

P.O. BOX 6249
Westlake Village, CA 91359

SECTION THREE

ROADMAPS

"Some programs are
more popular than others"

CHAPTER VII

EXAMPLES OF ACTUAL LOG ON SEQUENCES

* Basic Concept * Dym – The Most Popular?
* RCP/M – Downloading Example

Basic Concept

1	Setup	Computer Communications Program Modem Phone Line
2	Run Program	Enter terminal mode or follow specific instructions of your program.
3	Dial phone number	Choose a bulletin board to call. (Review menu if BBS is a known type)
4	Confirm modem answering on other end	Hear the high pitched tone. or see message on your screen if using a fancy modem.
5	Connect Up	Push the connect button or use whatever command your modem requires.
6	Log On	Answer all questions that the bulletin board asks you. Most log on procedures are very easy as they are self-documenting. Simply answer the questions the bulletin board asks and you're . . .

* * ON-LINE * * * ON-LINE * * * ON-LINE * * * ON-LINE * * * ON-LINE * *

COMPUTER DATING? – TRY IT THE DIAL YOUR MATCH WAY

It's Friday nite and you are pondering the usual choices for the evening's activities. What to do – Catch a movie?, Go to a disco?, Hit the bars? You opt to spend the evening at a friend's house playing with the computer. Your friend has been wanting to show you his new modem for weeks. He sits you in front of the computer, dials a number, and connects up to a Dial-Your-Match bulletin board. You log on as a new member and are immediately confronted with the following questionnaire . . . .

```
What is your FIRST name:
=> ANDREA

What CITY are you calling from:
=> LA

What is the 2 letter post office
abbreviation of the state you are
calling from:
=> CA

Your first name is: ANDREA
You're calling from: LA, CA

is that correct? => Y

How old are you ?
=> 28

What is your WEIGHT ?
=> 125

What is your HEIGHT (in INCHES) ?
=> 65

You are 28 years old
You weigh 125 pounds
and are 65 INCHES tall

Is that correct? => Y

What is your sex?
   A. Male
   B. Female
=> B
You picked: B

Female
Correct ?=> Y

Do you often have access to a computer
terminal, so you can answer your
electronic mail? If so, what kind?
   A. Yes,Apple
   B. Yes,Atari
   C. Yes,IBM-PC
   D. Yes,Commodore
   E. Yes,Radio Shack
   F. Yes,Heath/Zenith
   G. Yes,another brand of personal computer
   H. Yes,a mainframe terminal
   I. No,I am borrowing a friends
```

```
You picked: G
Yes,another brand of personal computer
Correct ?=> Y

What is the color of your EYES?
    A. eyes of brown
    B. eyes of blue
    C. hazel eyes
    D. eyes of green
    E. red eyes
    F. Betty Davis eyes
    G. Martian eyes!!
=> B
You picked: B
eyes of blue
Correct ?=> Y

What is the color of your HAIR?
    A. Brown hair
    B. Black hair
    C. Red hair
    D. I'm a Blond!
    E. Gray hair
    F. Auburn hair
    G. Hair? What hair?
    H. Antennae only!
=> D
You picked: D

I'm a Blond!
Correct ?=> Y

What is your marital status?
    A. Divorced
    B. Widowed
    C. Never married
    D. Married
    E. Married but available!
=> C
You picked: C

Never married

Correct ?=> Y

Current education level?
    A. Did not finish high school
    B. High school
    C. Some college or technical school
    D. 2 year degree
    E. 4 year degree
    F. Masters degree
    G. Doctorate
=> G
You picked: G
```

```
Doctorate
Correct ?=> Y

Do you have children?, and
how many live with you?
    A. Kids-NO! (Thank God!)
    B. Kids-Yes and none
    C. Kids-Yes and one
    D. Kids-Yes and two
    E. Kids-Yes and three or more
=> A
You picked: A

Kids-NO! (Thank God!)
Correct ?=> Y

How long have you resided
in your community?
    A. Newcomer
    B. Lived here 2 - 5 years
    C. Lived here over 5 years
=> A
You picked: A

Newcomer
Correct ?=> Y

How would others rate your appearance?
    A. A Fox!
    B. Very attractive
    C. Good looking
    D. Average
    E. Not too bad
    F. My mother loves me!
=> A
You picked: A

A Fox!
Correct ?=> Y

In a relationship.....
    A. Outside encounters are okay
    B. Both should be faithful
=> B
You picked: B

Both should be faithful
Correct ?=> Y

Do you have or like pets or animals?
    A. Yes, I have or like pets
    B. No, I do not like pets
=> A
You picked: A
```

```
Yes, I have or like pets
Correct ?=> Y

What is the importance of sex to you?
    A. Sex-I can take it or leave it
    B. Sex-A natural part of a relationship
    C. Sex-A constant requirement!
=> C
You picked: C

Sex-A constant requirement!
Correct ?=> Y

How do you feel about drugs?
    A. Drugs-They should only be taken if ill
    B. Drugs-Not for me...OK for others
    C. Moderate drug use is OK
    D. Recreational drugs enhance life
    E. I love getting high
=> A
You picked: A

Drugs-They should only be taken if ill
Correct ?=> Y

Are you a Football, Baseball fan, ETC?
    A. Yes, I'm a sports fan
    B. I like sports, but I'm not a fanatic
    C. No, I don't care for sports
=> B
You picked: B

I like sports, but I'm not a fanatic
Correct ?=> Y

Do you jog or work out occasionally?
    A. YES YES YES! I'm a health nut!
    B. Yes, I jog/work out occasionally
    C. No, I do not jog or work out
    D. Watching Richard Simmons makes me tired
=> B
You picked: B

Yes, I jog/work out occasionally
Correct ?=> Y

Do you smoke?
    A. Smoke cigarettes
    B. I don't smoke!
=> B
You picked: B

I don't smoke!
Correct ?=> Y
```

```
What are your views on drinking?
   A. People shouldn't drink
   B. Drinking helps me loosen up
   C. I like a drink now and then
   D. Drinking is okay for others
   E. I love drinking!
=> C
You picked: C

I like a drink now and then
Correct ?=> Y

What types of music do you like?
   A. Rock
   B. Punk
   C. New wave
   D. Country & Western
   E. Classical
   F. Jazz
   G. Rhythm & Blues
   H. Top 40
   I. Soul
   J. Opera
   K. Folk
   L. Disco
Pick up to 8 of the above and
enter them in the order of preference.
(Do NOT use commas or spaces!!)
=> ACDEF
You picked: ACDEF

Rock, New wave, Country & Western, Classical, Jazz
Correct ?=> Y

What are your hobbies/interests?
   A. Aviation
   B. Ham Radio
   C. Camping/Hiking
   D. Skiing
   E. Scuba diving
   F. Electronics
   G. Computers
   H. Gaming
   I. Sailing
   J. Photography
   K. Travel
   L. Theater
   M. Dancing
   N. Sports
   O. Stereo/Video
   P. Consulting
   Q. Software
Pick up to 8 of the above and
enter them in the order of preference.
(Do NOT use commas or spaces!!)
```

```
=> HIJDK
You picked: HIJDK

Gaming, Sailing, Photography, Skiing, Travel
Correct ?=> Y

-> Filing questionnaire. Please wait


Your ADDRESS CODE is:        (HERE YOU WILL BE ASSIGNED A SPECIFIC
                             ELECTRONIC MAIL ADDRESS. ITS IMPOR-
ANDREA XXXX                  TANT THAT YOU KEEP A RECORD OF AD-
                             DRESS CODES AND PASSWORDS FOR FU-
                             TURE ACCESS.)

Your ADDRESS CODE will be given out by
the computer to all persons that match
to you. You may also give it to people
wishing to send you private mail.

Your ADDRESS CODE is a combination of
your NAME and your FILE NUMBER.

The FILE NUMBER is used to identify
users when browsing and sending
private mail. You will also need your
FILE NUMBER when you log on again.
For security purposes you will be
asked to enter a four character
PASSWORD. The FILE NUMBER and PASSWORD
will be needed each time you log-on
so PLEASE write them down so you don't
forget them.

ENTER A 4 CHARACTER PASSWORD    (HERE YOU ENTER A PASSWORD
=> XXXX                           OF YOUR OWN CHOOSING)
```

After completing the answers, you are logged into the computer's database. You press M for "Make me a Match" and watch in disbelief as the names of potential friends and lovers scroll up the screen. You can browse the questionaires of people who interest you (they can also browse through your answers). You also have the option to leave electronic mail for them if you like. Futureworld? No, its here now.

Although DYMs are mostly used as dating boards, they have the potential to bring together people for any purpose. The DYM program was brought to life in late 1981 in Burbank, Ca., by programmer Gregg Collins. The basic concept is to allow people to seek out and find others with similar life interests, problems, and desires. The relative anonimity of telecomputing allows people the opportunity to reveal their personality without fear of physical rejection based on appearance and first impressions. Ironically, the computer is being used to help humans communicate their needs and emotions to each other — something we often find difficult if not impossible to do face-to-face.

Dial-Your-Match bulletin board systems are among the most frequently accessed systems around. The tremendous popularity of these boards points out the basic human need for reaching out and making contact with other humans who have similar interests. In fact, these boards are so popular that a modem with automatic re-dial capability may be a NECESSITY if you become an addicted user.

RCP/M Log on

RCP/M boards are run in many different ways. Most allow downloading of public domain software. This example is from an RCP/M bulletin board running ZCPR2. Commands may differ slightly from system to system. Procedures for downloading, however, are similar on most RCP/M boards. Pay attention to messages and documentation you will find on the boards themselves for details.

AFTER DIALING AN RCP/M BOARD AND HOOKING IN YOU WILL SEE SOMETHING LIKE THE FOLLOWING:

```
You are caller #  3355
Next msg # will be  383

Function (B,E,R,S,K,G,W,C,U,P,X,Q (or '?' if not known)  ?

Functions supported:
S--> Scan messages      R--> Retrieve message
E--> Enter message      K--> Kill message
B--> retype Bulletins   W--> retype welcome
C--> exit to CP/M       U--> list User file
P--> Prompt (bel) togl  X--> eXpert user mode
Q--> Quick summary      G--> Goodbye (signoff)

Commands may be strung together, separated by semicolons.
For example, 'R;123' retrieves message # 123.
You can also use 'R;1+' to retrieve all msgs starting at # 1...

Software exchange is done under CP/M using
the XMODEM program (for intelligent transfer)
or the TYPE command (simple ASCII listing).

Use CHAT under CP/M to talk with the SYSOP...

Function (B,E,R,S,K,G,W,C,U,P,X,Q (or '?' if not known)? [C]

To get directory of ALL files (ALL user areas/BOTH disks):
   A0>DIR A: $ADL

To re-enter RBBS, type:
   A0>RBBS

To disconnect:
   A0>BYE     (use if you want to leave comments to sysop on exit)
   A0>BYE/F  (quick logoff)
```

```
For additional information and tips:
    A0>HELP   (use control-C to exit HELP when finished)

Entering CP/M...

ZCPR2

A0>[help]
HELP for ZCPR2, Version 4.0

Default HELP Facility Invoked
        Available HELP Files are --
HELP
        Type Any Character for Default Info (^C to Abort) -[cr]

  HELP File Selections are --
A.  Named directory map
B.  Changing disk/user
C.  Directory of all files
D.  Re-entering RBBS
E.  Disconnecting
F.  Talk with sysop
G.  Downloading
H.  Looking at library files

Type  ^C=CP/M or Enter Selection a

:PWD

To get named directory map (print working directories):
    A0>PWD DIR
    (This will display the directory names and the
    name of your current working directory)
    (Type PWD // for info on PWD.)
    (The names are used by CD to change disk/user,
    use DIR for a directory of files.


Type  ^C=CP/M or Enter Selection b

:CD

To change disk/user area:
    A0>B:
    B0>1:
    B1>A2:
    A2>  (... etc.)
    (use "du:" form to switch user areas. (A0: - B8:))
  or
    A0>CD dirname
    (Where "dirname" is one of the directory names listed
    by PWD DIR. Type CD // for info on CD.)

    (Also type USER for more info on named disk/user areas)

Type  ^C=CP/M or Enter Selection c
```

:DIR

To get directory listings of all files:
    A0>DIR A: $ADLN
    (Currently, only two drives A: and B:, only users 0 and 1,
    have files. Disk B: contents will be changed periodically
    to make up for lack of on-line space. Leave requests for
    files you wish to download on the bulletin board.. If I
    have it off-line, I'll stick on drive B:) (The "L" option
    lists library member files.)

Type   ^C=CP/M or Enter Selection d

:RBBS

To re-enter bulletin board:
    A0>RBBS
    (You won't have to log on again, as system "remembers"
    who you are.)

Type   ^C=CP/M or Enter Selection e

:BYE

To disconnect:
    A0>BYE
    (OR you can re-enter RBBS and use the "G" option,
    which you should do if you want to leave comments
    to sysop on signoff.)

Type   ^C=CP/M or Enter Selection f

:CHAT

To talk with SYSOP:

    A0>CHAT
    (If I'm around, which is not too often...)

Type   ^C=CP/M or Enter Selection g

:XMODEM/TYPE

To transfer files:
    Use XMODEM (for Christensen protocol)
     Public files are uploaded to drive B:, user 0.
     Private files are uploaded to drive B:, user 9.
     The "L" option will let you download a selected
     file contained within a library file.
     (Use the "PR" or "PRC" options instead of "R" or "RC"
     for private uploads.) (Type XMODEM // for examples.)
  or
    TYPE (for XON/XOFF (ctrl-Q/ctrl-S) protocol)
     (TYPE on this system works on squeezed files as well as
     unsqueezed, and also supports wildcards for multiple
     file listings.) (Use LTYPE for library files.)

```
          (Note that you must use XMODEM for .OBJ and other
          binary data files.)


Type   ^C=CP/M or Enter Selection h

:LTYPE

To preview files within a library:
     A0>LTYPE libname filename
     (Where "libname"=library file, "filename"=file in library)
     (Will unsqueeze file if squeezed, but only shows the
     first 80 lines, use XMODEM L to get the whole thing)
     (Use DIR libname $L to get listing of files in a library.)

Type   ^C=CP/M or Enter Selection [^c]
```

         THE ABOVE ILLUSTRATES A TYPICAL LOG ON AND THEN A PERUSAL OF
THE HELP FILES. TO FIND OUT WHICH FILES AND PROGRAMS ARE CUR-
RENTLY AVAILABLE TO BE DOWNLOADED FROM THE SYSTEM, CHECK THE
DIRECTORY:

```
A0>dir a: $adl


-RBBS.    0k | BYE   .COM 16k | CD  .COM 4k | CHAT    .COM   1k
HELP .COM 3k | LTYPE .COM  9k | PWD .COM 5k | RBBS    .COM  35k
XMODEM  .COM   6k
    >>> Drive A, user 0 contains 79k in 9 files with 11k free.

-UPLOADS. 0k | DECHEX .OBJ 4k | DISK76F.LBR 6k | LU300 .OBJ 19k
RECVER21.OBJ   4k
    > Library file members for B0:DISK76F .LBR
DISK7   .DQC  16s | DISK76F .COM  31s |
    > This library contains 47 sectors.
    >> 2 member files in 1 library(s) with 47 sectors total.
    >>> Drive B, user 0 contains 33k in 5 files with 51k free.

-RCPMLIS.T   0k | ACNODE  .DOC 1k | HAWAII  .BBS 1k | RCPM-040.LQT 15k
RCPM-SYS.OPS 3k | RCPM3940.DQF 4k | RCPMLIST.DQC 3k | RCPMLIST.UPD 1k
    >>> Drive B, user 1 contains 28k in 8 files with 51k free.

-KAYPRO. 0k | KCLOCK.DOC 2k | KPRO-DSK.FIX 1k | KPRO-VID.FIX  1k
KSPEED .DOC   2k | KZ2     .LBR 64k | SPEED    .DOC   3k
    > Library file members for B3:KZ2      .LBR
DIR.COM 28s   | GENINS.COM  98s  | KZ2.COM 62s | KZ2    .DQC  63s
SD-60.DQC 58s | STARTUP.COM 30s   | TYPE.COM 71s | WHEEL .COM   11s

ZCPRHDR.LQB 81s |
    > This library contains 502 sectors.
    >> 9 member files in 1 library(s) with 502 sectors total.
    >>> Drive B, user 3 contains 73k in 7 files with 51k free.

A0>b:(cr)
```

TYPICAL DOWNLOADING PROCEDURE

The following shows how the program "recver21.obj" was downloaded from an RCP/M board using a version of Modem7. The commands in brackets ([]) show what was actually typed at the keyboard.

DESCRIPTION

1. Request the bulletin board to send file "recver21.obj"

2. The xmodem program on the BBS opens the file and show how long it will take to transfer.

3. On most versions of Modem7, you must now leave terminal mode by typing Control-E (be sure to save anything in the buffer by using the command WRT or NOL).

4. Next, tell get your computer ready to receive the program "recver21.obj" and store it on disk b.

5. Your computer will then inform you of the progress of the file transfer by showing the blocks being received. When the transfer is completed return to terminal mode ("T" on most versions).

6. At this point you can continue to download other programs and files or you can return to the message section of the board by typing "RBBS"

ACTUAL SEQUENCE

```
B0>[xmodem s recver21.obj(cr)]


XMODEM v7.4
File open: 26 (001AH) records
Send time: 2 mins, 0 secs at 300
To cancel: use CTL-X

[Control-E] or whatever command
your program uses to get back
into command mode from terminal
mode.


COMMAND[:[r b:recver21.obj(cr)]
```

```
Welcome back, TOM BEESTON...

Active # of msg's  60.
You are caller #  3356
Next msg # will be  383

AND NOW FOR THE LOG OFF:

Function (B,E,R,S,K,G,W,C,U,P,X,Q (or '?' if not known)? [g]

OK to disconnect? (HANG UP) (Y/N)? [y]

Want to leave any comments? (Y/N)? y

Enter comments; to end, hit C/R.
   <-------------------- MAX LINE LENGTH -------------------->
Ok> kim-thanks again for letting us use your board in the book!-t
Ok>

...from Kim Levitt: Thanks for calling, TOM.

ZCPR2

Good-bye...
```

"Find a Date,
Meet your Mate!"

NOTES:

CHAPTER VIII
SAMPLE BBS MENUS

ABBS

APPLE BULLETIN-BOARD SYSTEM

Software for this program runs exclusively on the Apple II system, but any system can call in.

WELCOME TO THE APPLE BULLETIN BOARD SYSTEM OF ANY CITY, ANYWHERE

> > >—BULLETINS—< < < <

NEXT MESSAGE WILL BE # 2255

FUNCTIONS SUPPORTED:

A = APPLE 40 COLUMN
B = PRINT BULLETIN
D = DUPLEX SWITCH (ECHO/NO ECHO)
E = ENTER MSG INTO SYSTEM
G = GOOD-BYE (LEAVE SYSTEM)
H = HELP WITH FUNCTIONS
K = KILL (ERASE) A MESSAGE
L = LINE FEED (ON/OFF)
N = NULLS (SET AS REQ'D)
Q = QUICK SUMMARY OF SUBJS
R = RETRIEVE MSG
S = MESSAGES
T = TIME AND DATE
V = VIDEO MODE (ON/OFF)
W = PRINTS WELCOME MESSAGE
X = EXPERT USER
? = PRINTS FUNCTIONS SUPPORTED

FOLLOWING IS A BRIEF LIST AND DESCRIPTION OF THE COMMANDS AND THEIR USAGE:

CTRL E – RETYPES CURRENT LINE UP TO PRE SENT POSITION AND ALLOWS YOU TO CONTINUE FROM THAT POINT.

CTRL H (BACKSPACE) **–** ALLOWS YOU TO BACK SPACE ONE CHARACTER AT A TIME AND PRINTS A '\' FOLLOWED BY THE CHARACTER YOU ARE BACK-SPACING OVER. THIS IS THE SAME ROUTINE AS IS USED FOR DELETE OR RUBOUT INSTEAD OF TRUE DELETE. (FOR THE BENEFIT OF PRINTERS)

CTRL U (FORWARD ARROW) **–** STARTS YOU BACK AT THE BEGINNING OF THE CURRENT LINE BEING TYPED. (I.E. START OVER)

A – APPLE 40 COLUMN. NORMALLY YOU WOULD BE ALLOWED 64 CHAR-ACTERS PER LINE. A BELL WILL SOUND AT 59 AND ON UP TO 64 COLUMNS AT WHICH POINT YOU WOULD BE FORCED ONTO THE NEXT LINE OF TEXT. IN THE APPLE 40 MODE RING AT 35 DROPPING YOU TO THE NEXT LINE AT 39. 39 WAS USED INSTEAD OF 40 TO AVOID AN EXTRA BLANK LINE BE-CAUSE OF THE 40 TH CHARACTER.

B – PRINT BULLETIN. PRINTS BULLETINS AT BEGINNING OF PROGRAM.

D – DUPLEX SWITCH. ALTERNATELY SELECTS FULL OR HALF DUPLEX OPER-ATION AND IN FORMS YOU OF CURRENT STATUS.

E – ENTER MESSAGE. ALLOWS YOU TO ENTER A MESSAGE INTO SYSTEM. ENTER COMMANDS ARE BASICALLY SELF EXPLANATORY. A CARRIAGE RE-TURN (C/R) AT THIS POINT WILL LIST OUT THE COMMAND MENU FOR EN-TRIES. THE CHANGE COMMAND ALLOW YOU TO CHANGE AN ENTIRE LINE BUT NOT JUST CHANGE PART OF IT. MAKE SURE WHY YOU ARE DONE WITH THE MESSAGE TO SAVE IT TO DISC WITH THE 'S' COMMAND.

G – GOODBYE. EXIT PROGRAM.

H – HELP. PRINTS THIS ROUTINE.

K – KILL A MESSAGE. ENTER THIS TO DELETE A MESSAGE FROM THE FILE. A PASS WORD MAY BE NECESSARY IF ONE WAS USED AT THE TIME OF MES-SAGE ENTRY.

L – LINE FEED ON/OFF. NORMALLY ON. FOR TERMINALS THAT NEED AN EXTRA LINE FEED CHARACTER TO ADVANCE TO THE NEXT LINE.

N – NULLS. ADDS AN EXTRA DELAY AFTER A CARRIAGE RETURN TO ALLOW PRINTERS TIME TO MOVE THE PRINTERHEAD BACK TO STARTING POSI-TION. THIS OPTION ONLY WORKS WITH THE LINE FEED OPTION ON. EACH NULL IS EQUIVALENT TO 30 MILLISECONDS DELAY AND IS ADJUSTABLE FROM 1 TO 30. IT DEFAULTS TO ONE.

Q – QUICK SCAN. AN ABBREVIATED SCAN. SEE 'S'

R – RETRIEVE MESSAGES. ALLOWS YOU TO RETRIEVE A MESSAGE FROM THE FILE.

S – SUMMARIZE MESSAGES. ALLOWS YOU TO SCAN OVER MESSAGES STARTING AT THE MESSAGE # YOU SPECIFY.

T – TIME AND DATE. GIVES YOU THE CURRENT TIME AND DATE. THIS IS ALSO USED AUTOMATICALLY DURING LOG-IN.

W – WELCOME. PRINTS WELCOME MESSAGE AT BEGINNING OF PROGRAM.

X – EXPERT USER. DOES AWAY WITH CERTAIN EXPLANATORY MESSAGES DURING THE PROGRAM. IT ALSO ALLOWS CERTAIN C/R DEFAULTS. EX FUNCTIONS? WILL PRINT FUNCTIONS SUPPORTED BY THE SYSTEM.

— PRINTS FUNCTIONS SUPPORTED IN THAT CURRENT MODE OF OPERATION.

A-C-C-E-S-S

This program also runs on an Apple (but most computers can call in)

★ ★
WELCOME TO
AN A-C-C-E-S-S SYSTEM
★ ★

TYPE '<CTRL.> N' AT ANY TIME
TO GET 5 NULLS AFTER EACH <C/R>.
– –
USE THE CATEGORY 'MAIL' FOR MESSAGES TO A SPECIFIC PERSON.
MAIL SYSTEM SUGGESTIONS OR COMMENTS TO 'OPERATOR'. (ENTER AS
FIRST NAME).
– –
TYPE 'H' IN RESPONSE TO THE 'FUNCTION:'
PROMPT FOR HELP WITH THE FUNCTIONS OR
FOR TIME SAVING TIPS.
– –
this line is lower case.
IF YOU CANNOT READ THE ABOVE LINE THEN
TYPE A 'C' AT THE 'FUNCTION:' PROMPT.
★ ★

NEXT MESSAGE WILL BE # 10026

Functions Supported:

A = APPLE 40/STANDARD 80 COLUMN MODE
B = BULLETINS
C = CASE (UPPER ONLY/UPPER & lower)
D = DUPLEX SWITCH (ECHO/NO ECHO)
E = ENTER MSG. INTO SYSTEM
F = FIND A SUBJECT (SEARCH)
G = GOOD BYE (LEAVE SYSTEM)
H = HELP WITH FUNCTIONS
I = INFORMATION
K = KILL (ERASE) A MESSAGE
L = LINE FEED (ON/OFF)
M = MAIL (SEND/RETRIEVE)
N = NULLS (SET AS REQD.)
O = OTHER SYSTEMS
P = PRINTING/VIDEO TERMINAL MODE
Q = QUICK SCAN OF MESSAGES
R = RETRIEVE MESSAGES
S = SCAN MESSAGES
T = TIME AND DATE
U = UPDATE (CHANGE) EXISTING MESSAGE
W = WELCOME MESSAGE
X = EXPERT/BEGINNER MODE
# = FORMS AND ORDERS
? = LISTS FUNCTIONS SUPPORTED

FUNCTION:(TYPE '?' FOR LIST OF AVAILABLE FUNCTIONS) ??

Functions Supported:

A = APPLE 40/STANDARD 80 COLUMN MODE
B = BULLETINS
C = CASE (UPPER ONLY/UPPER & lower)
D = DUPLEX SWITCH (ECHO/NO ECHO)
E = ENTER MSG. INTO SYSTEM
F = FIND A SUBJECT (SEARCH)
G = GOOD BYE (LEAVE SYSTEM)
H = HELP WITH FUNCTIONS
I = INFORMATION
K = KILL (ERASE) A MESSAGE
L = LINE FEED (ON/OFF)
M = MAIL (SEND/RETRIEVE)
N = NULLS (SET AS REQD.)
O = OTHER SYSTEMS
P = PRINTING/VIDEO TERMINAL MODE
Q = QUICK SCAN OF MESSAGES
R = RETRIEVE MESSAGES
S = SCAN MESSAGES
T = TIME AND DATE

U = UPDATE (CHANGE) EXISTING MESSAGE
W = WELCOME MESSAGE
X = EXPERT/BEGINNER MODE
# = FORMS AND ORDERS
? = LISTS FUNCTIONS SUPPORTED

FUNCTION:(TYPE '?' FOR LIST OF AVAILABLE FUNCTIONS) ?H

Enter function you desire help with, or Enter 'CTRL' for control characters, or Enter 'ALL' for complete review. (Ctrl. 'S' stops output, any other key resumes)

<CTRL> 'C' — Aborts current line being printed and continues on next line.

<CTRL> 'E' — Retypes current line up to present position and allows you to continue from that point.

<CTRL> 'H' (Backspace) — Allows you to backspace one character at a time and if you are in printing terminal mode it prints a '\' followed by the character you are backspacing over.

<CTRL> 'K' — Kills current function and takes you to the next step.

<CTRL> 'N' — Configures system to send 5 null characters after each carriage return to allow printers time to return the printhead to the beginning of the line. This may be typed at any time during output.

<CTRL> 'R' — Flags message for later retrieval during a Scan (S), Quick Scan (Q) or Find (F) command. The message that is flagged is the one that was printed previous to the one currently being printed. See 'R' for retrieval of msgs.

<CTRL> 'S' — Stops scrolling (Freezes output) until any other key is hit.

<CTRL> 'U' (Forward arrow) — Starts you back at the beginning of the current line being typed. (i.e. Start over).

<CTRL> 'X' — Kills current function and returns you to 'FUNCTION:' prompt.

A — Apple 40 column mode. You are allowed 80 characters per line when entering a message. The bell will sound at 75-80 columns, forcing you to a new line after 80. In the apple 40 column mode, the bell will also sound at the 39th. column and on msg. retrieval formats output for 40 columns, preventing word splitting.
B — Bulletin. Prints bulletins at beginning of program.

C — Case switch. Alternately selects UPPER CASE ONLY or UPPER/lower case mode of operation and informs you of current status.

D — Duplex switch. Alternately selects full or half duplex operation and informs you of current status.

E – Enter message. Allows you to enter a message into the system. Commands are basically self explanatory. A carriage return <C/R> alone on a line when entering text will list out the commands for entries. A '?' at this point will list the command menu. An 'H' will describe the commands. Make sure when you are done with the message to save it to disk with the 'S' command.

F – Find. Searches subjects for a particular word and lists the message no's. in which that word was found.

G – Goodbye. Exit program.

H – Help. Prints a description of the commands and their usage. 'H' may also be typed at the message entry level prompt for a description of the message entry level functions.

I – Information. Gives information about this system.

K – Kill a message. Enter this to de lete a message from the file. A password may be necessary if one was used at the time of message entry.

L – Line feed on/off. Normally on. For terminals that need a line feed character to advance to a new line.

M – Mail. Allows you to retrieve messages directed specifically to you, or to send a message to a specific person. Mail can be retrieved only by the addressee.

N – Nulls. Adds an extra delay after a carriage return to allow printers time to move the printhead back to the starting position. Each null is equivalent to 30 milliseconds delay and is adjustable from 0 to 40. It defaults to 0. A <CTRL>'N' sets it to 5 and can be typed at any time.

O – Other systems. Prints a list of other message type systems.

P – Printing terminal mode. Prints a '\' followed by character you are backspacing over when in this mode. Normally in Video terminal mode.

Q – Quick scan. An abbreviated scan. see 'S'.

R – Retrieve messages. Allows you to retrieve a message from the file. An 'R' followed by a carriage return will prompt you for the message you wish to retrieve. Multiple messages may be retrieved by separating the message numbers with a semi-colon (;). An 'R' followed by the message number(s) wil, retrieve the specified message(s). (Ex. 'R7;15' will retrieve messages 7 and 15). They may be retrieved in any order. Typing 'R*' will retrieve messages flagged during a Scan (S), Quick scan (Q), or Find (F). See <**CTRL**>'R'.

S – Scan messages. Allows you to scan over messages in a specific category starting at the message # you specify. Entering a negative number will scan backward.

T – Time and date. Gives the current time and date and the time you have spent on the system.

U – Update existing message. Enter this to change a message you have previously entered. Messages to a specific person can not be changed.

W – Welcome. Prints welcome message seen at beginning of program.

X – Expert user. Does away with certain explanatory messages during the program.

 # – Allows you to fill out a prepared form. A list of forms may be obtained by typing a '?' at the 'Form:' prompt When finished enter a '?' for a list of message entry commands.

? – Prints functions supported in that current mode of operation. A '?' in response to 'Category:' prints a list of possible categories.

Enter function you desire help with, or Enter 'CTRL' for control characters, or Enter 'ALL' for complete review. (Ctrl. 'S' stops output, any other key resumes). <C/R> to return to 'FUNCTION:' prompt.

BULLET-80

This program runs on a TRS-80. Again any computer can call in.

Good Afternoon, Welcome to Bullet-80 Version 8.0(a) c. 1983, Computer Services Of Danbury, Danbury Ct.

NOTE: Pressing <ENTER> from an abbreviated menu expands it Use option <D> from Main Menu for complete instructions. To Read System Bulletins Use <B> From Main Menu Use Option <A> From Main Menu To Activate Private Password

These Are The Commands That Can Be Used:

<**A**>utolog	<**B**>ulletins
<**D**>irections	<**F**>ile-Transfer
<**H**>ow-Long	<**M**>essage-Base
<**N**>ew-Messages	<**O**>ther-Numbers
<**R**>equest-Chat	<**S**>ystem-Config <**T**>erminate
<**U**>sers-Log	<**V**>iew-System
<**X**>pert-User	

Your Choice ? Directions

Bullet-80 System Directions

Press <S> To Stop, Ctrl-S Or <P> To Pause

Most command inputs in Bullet-80 are INKEY$ functions, you do not need to press <ENTER> when entering the command. Entering a Carriage Return, <C/R>, or pressing <ENTER> at an abbreviated menu will display an expanded menu if you're not sure what to do. Note ** You Can Also Press <S> To Stop Or Control-S Or <P> To Pause During The Print-Out Of Module Instructions, and while reading messages. Any Input Will Restart The Display.

Here is an explaination of the commands :

<A>utolog – Allows you to register an auto-logon password which becomes active immediatly.

<B>ulletins – This command will display the current system <B>ulletins.

<C>lub – Not active on this Bullet-80.

<D>irections – The instructions you are now reading.

<E>lectronic Shopping – Not active on this Bullet-80.

<F>ile Transfer – This command gives you access to: <D>ownloading, <U>ploading, and <P>rogram Transfer. Bullet-80 supports Standard ASCII, DFT, XFER/CMD, Xmodem and Modem file transfers.

Download – This module allows you to get programs from our database. There are six download menu's, which are changed each Monday morning.

Program Uploading – This module will allow you to upload your ORIGINAL or PUBLIC DOMAIN programs to Bullet-80. After review they will be added to one of the download menus.

Program Transfer – This module allows users to transfer a program from one to another privately. Complete instructions are available from the module menu.

<G> ames – Not active on this Bullet-8p.

<H>ow Long – This function will tell you how long you've been on Bullet-80 for this session. It will also give you the current local time and date.

<I>nterests – This module will allow you to enter any interests or hobbies you have, or things you like to do. This information will be made available to other Bullet-80 users to read and see if you have anything in common. This module is NOT ACTIVE on this system, but may be added if there is sufficient interest.

<M>essage Base – This module is where you gain access to the Messages on Bullet-80. Here you have the option of <R>eading, <S>canning, or <L>eaving mail

for Bullet-80's other users. Each section of the message center has help menus for full instructions.

<O>ther Network Phone Numbers – Prints out a list of many on-line systems. This option allows you to search for any BBS by city, state, area code, or network name. If you know of any not listed, leave me a message as you terminate and I will add it.

<R>equest CHAT – This will allow you to chat with the sysop via the TRS-80. If he's not available within about 1 minute, you will be returned to the main menu. You may also leave him a private message as you terminate.

<S>ystem Config – This function lets you to customize Bullet-80 to your terminal by letting you adjust screen width, line feeds, upper and lower case, nulls and your bell code. These settings are only active during the current session.

<T>erminate – Logs you off of Bullet-80. At this time you can leave a private message to the Sysop, if desired.

<U>sers Log - Will display Bullet-80 users for you. You can scan <F>orward, <R>everse or <S>earch by name.

<V>iew System Configuration – Will tell you about the hardware and software used on this Bullet-80.

<X>pert User – The first time you call Bullet-80 you will be considered a novice user and all menu's will be printed out in full. On all future calls you will be an expert with short menus You always have the option of toggling your <X>pert status with the <X> command.

CBBS

This board was one of the first in existence. It is run by two of the pioneers of home telecomputing – Ward Christensen and Randy Suess.

Welcome updated 12/03/82; CBBS(R)/Chicago (312) 545-8086
    Terminal need nulls? Type "N" while this types:
—> Tired of seeing welcome? Press "c" to skip it.

** WELCOME TO WARD AND RANDY'S
** COMPUTERIZED BULLETIN BOARD SYSTEM (R) (C.B.B.S. (R))
** (In operation since 2/16/78)

—> PRESS "S" TO STOP OUTPUT, "S" TO START IT AGAIN <—
    (NO DATA WILL BE LOST)

CONTROL CHARACTERS ACCEPTED BY CBBS:

ASCII CHARS	CTL CHARS	
	DEL/BS	Character delete
C	C	Cancel output (*)
	I	Tab (Tabs set every 8)
K	K	Function abort (*)
N	N	Send 5 more nulls (*)
	R	Retype input line
S	S	Stop/start output (*)
ESC	U	Line delete
	W	video Word backspace
	X	Video line delete

(*): Use while CBBS types to you. If you get stuck, try: Ctl-K then C/R until you bail out back to the main menu.

Whenever we refer to "C/R", we mean your "return" key!!

"FRILLS": CTL-L shows length of input field; CTL-E types a C/R back to you, but doesn't end the line you are keying. Use ";" to separate multiple answers, i.e.
    n;firstname;lastname;x;p;
would log you in, set video mode, expert mode, no prompt bells.

——END OF WELCOME——

—> BULLETINS: 29 lines, last entry 07/83, newest entries 1st

Press "C" to skip 1 bulletin. Repeat as desired. K skips everything.

—> 07/28/82 1200 baud online with UDS modem and North Star 4-port serial board, that only supports 110, 300, 600, and 1200. (A)lter baud rate command is temporarily unavailable.

CBBS policy:
• Hobby computing, ham, electronics hobbyist msgs welcome.
• Commercial msgs in above areas welcome
• Pers. msgs between hobbyists/hams OK.
• Please use your real name. (Other msgs deleted)
• Please don't leave #'s/passwords for non-public systems. or offer to trade such passwords.
• Please don't offer to buy/sell/trade personal copies of licensed software you have purchased for a single user.

—> Msgs 1-19 = info. of general interest; 20-29 = local clubs
• Periodically updated
• Type q;1 or s;1 then when you've seen enough, press K to stop the summary.

MINOR FUNCTIONS: Press K-to abort

# Print caller # etc	(P)rompt bell off	(U)ser update (password, etc)
(A) (not available)	(K)ill message	(V)ideo backspace
(B)ulletin reprint	(N)ulls: How many?	(W)elcome reprint
(C)ase upper/lower	(O)ne line summary	e(X)pert user mode
(D)uplex: echo off	(T)ime/date/E.T.	

>> For details, type H, press return, then type the command letter. <<

CHAT See if Randy is available to talk via keyboard. (Please don't abuse this for "hi, how are you" – its meant to be used to report bugs, seek advice on CBBS usage, etc.)

HELP New user help; (vs. H: keyword based help)

MINE find my messages NEWS What's new on CBBS (Last updated 7/26/83)

SHORT Shorten output: no dup spaces, etc

New users: If you don't know what else to do, start with: S;1 or q;1 for quick subject-only summary. If short on time, or to only see new msgs, o;-50 or shorter yet: q;-50

COMMODORE

This board runs on the Commodore Computers

Commodore Public Bulletin Board
_____

Operated by: Commodore Midwest
Written by: Steve Punter

Commands Available on the System:

Type 'S' to stop the listing. Once stopped, 'S' will restart, 'A' will abort.

HELP – Reprint this list
A – Read All messages
B – Enter Bulletin area
C – Continue Reading
NEW – Read New messages
RALL – Read Messages Sent to ALL
F[#] – Forward Message Reading
R[#] – Reverse Message Reading
R – Recall a specific message
S – Summary of Available Messages
S[#] – Summary from Specific Msg
O – Overview of messages
O[#] – Overview from Specific Msg
TO – List message recipients
TOME – List messages sent to YOU
READ – Read messages sent to YOU

MINE – List messages YOU sent
FROM – List Messages FROM a User
E – Enter a message
F – Forward a message
P – Reply to last message
DM – Delete a message
LOAD – Load a program to your system
STAT – Display Transfer Stats
DP – Delete program
TIME – Display Time
EXP - Turn on Expert Mode
LF – Turn Off/On Line Feeds
DUP - Change Echoplex
LOG - System Usage Log
PLOG – Program Download Log
U - User Log
CONT – Toggle Continuous Mode
QUIT – Leave System
G - Goodbye (same as QUIT)
07/13/83

----

64 TERMINAL SOFTWARE

The revised versions of the Commodore 64 Terminal Program that supports Up and Downloading to this and other Punter BBS systems is available for downloading from this system. You will of course have to have another system to download the program with if you don't already have the 64 program. (And if you already have it, why download it anyway?) The program names are TERMINAL C-64 and TERM.64. You will need to download both parts.

To run the program, load and run TERMINAL C-64. This program will load the other module.

DYM

See the previous chapter for an example of a DYM log on.

    A – Answer change
    B –> Browse questionnaires
    C –> Chat with the Sysop

F –> Facts about this system
G –> Goodbye
I –> Immediate hang-up
L – > Library subsystem
M –> Match up users
O –> Other BBS systems
P –> Public message board
R –> Read private mail
S –> Send private mail
U –> User log display
V –> Adds and Valuable coupons
X –> Exit and LOGON again
? –> list commands

PMS

PMS stands for Peoples Message System and was written by Bill Blue. It runs on Apple computers.

WELCOME TO * PMS * LOS ANGELES, CA.

——>> System Commands

E = Enter a message into system.
F = Features, articles, excerpts.
G = Goodbye. Leave system. (hangup)
H = Help with various functions.
I = Information about system.
K = Kill a message from the files.
M = Message alert. Messages for you?
N = News – System news.
O = Other systems current summary.
Q = Quickscan of message headers.
R = Retrieve a message from the files.
S = Scan of message headers.
SR = Selective message retrieval.
T = Time, date and connect time.
U = User modifiable system functions.
X = eXpert user mode. (on/off toggle)
Z = Continue message entry after abort
? = Prints this list of commands.
***** = Flagged message memory retrieval.
TALK = Page sysop (if available)
TEST = Modem continuous test loop.
NEWCALL = Information for new callers.
GENERAL = UP/DN-LOAD (Open to all)

> * * System Control functions and codes **

There are certain characters which cause specific functions to occur while system is printing to you. (NOT when waiting for input. These may be control, lower or upper case characters.

– C – Stops printing the current line up to carriage return. Use this if you want to skip over several lines of text without aborting the function. Use one 'C' for each line you want to jump over.

– K – Causes a jump to the next logical operation. As an example, if you were retrieving several messages, it would cause a jump to the next message. During message entry listing, will return you to the message entry entry command level. The ONLY time this command will return to to main COMMAND level is if there is no logical next function. It can also be used to cancel the bulletins at sign-on, and jump directly to the message alert routine. (Two K's during bulletins would cancel bulletins and message alert and go right to COMMAND.

– N – Adds two nulls for each N typed. Use this when you have a printer online, which needs nulls (is dropping first characters of lines). May be used at any time in system operation. Another Use of this function would be to slow down a Scan or Quickscan if you are having trouble keeping up with it. See also 'P'.

– P – Cancels nulls to zero. Regardless of current null setting, resets nulls to zero. You can then add again with N if you wish.

– R – Flags messages during a scan or quickscan to be later retrieved with the * command. Type an R at the NEXT message header. It will always be one message behind. There is usually not time to comprehend a message header and type the R before that header is done being printed. So just pause slightly and then type it. At the end of that next header, you will get verification and number of the message flagged.

– S – Stops text output until any other character is sent.

– X – This guy causes an unconditional abort of whatever function you're in, and an immediate jump to main COMMAND level.

> * * System Commands * *

All system commands are input to the main COMMAND level. Certain commands, H,K,R and S may also have extenders describing or anticipating the next question asked. As an example: Since H is for help, if you wanted help on everything, you could type H;ALL. Using R as another example, if you wanted to retrieve message # 1937 you could type R;1937 etc. More examples of various multiple parameters are explained for each individual command.

(70)

– B – Reprints the bulletins that are displayed when you first sign on to the system.

– E – Enter a message into the system. Pretty self explanatory, just follow the prompting. You must enter a password when asked. This is the password used to kill the message. There are also two levels of security messages available. If you type LOCK as your password (you will be asked again for the password for killing), the message will be marked as private, and will automatically open for the person to whom its addressed or to who wrote it. Others will be asked for a password which will be the same as the password for killing it. If you enter LOCX instead of LOCK, the message can be read ONLY with the password.

– G – Goodbye. Exit the system and hangup the phone. Files will be updated at this time. System will also respond to: END, OFF, BYE and a few others.

– H – System help files. Typing an H by itself will print out all the possible areas you obtain help for. Typing H;(character) will print help on a specific function.

– K – Kill a message. This will remove a message from the system files. You must have the password (entered during message entry) to use this. You also have the option of automatically killing messages that are addressed to you at the time you read them. See more details in R command.

– M – Message alert. This command is issued automatically directly after the bulletins when you sign on. It allows you to automatically retrieve all messages addressed to you. You may use it at anytime in the program. One word of caution: If you have flagged messages for retrieval and use this command all the flagged messages will be lost. If you do use it, and did not retrieve all the messages to you, you can continue with the * command. (Same as flagged retrieval).

– O – Other systems list. Updated regularly, contains a summary of all know public access message systems of all types, in alphabetical order. Can also be printer formatted.

– Q – Quickscan of message headers. Not that much quicker. See also, S.

– R – Retrieve a messages from the files. There are several modes here. You can select messages singly, or in multiples. Examples of entries: R;381 or R381 or R381;560;etc.

   To retrieval all messages starting from a certain point, type: R;555^ or R;1010+. See also the * command for flagged msgs. When you retrieve a message that is addressed to you, at the end of it, you'll be asked if you want to kill it (automatically), and then if you want to reply to it. The automatic reply does some of the busywork for you (To: From: etc.) and upon completion of the reply and saving the message, will continue with retrieving other messages you may have specified. During auto-reply, if you just type carriage return in response to Subject?, it will take the subject of the message that was to you and add a R/ to it, meaning reply to:.

– S – Scan message headers. Here you can specify a starting message number to start the scan. S;500 would scan starting at message 500 or the next highest if there is no message 500. You can also scan in reverse order by either specifying a number > = the highest message number, or by adding a ' – ' (minus) sign directly after the message number. Examples: S;500 S1200 S;1040- etc. As you are scanning you use 'R' to flag messages you want to read later with the * command. See *.

– SR– Selective retrieval. Use this command to retrieve all messages whose headers contain data you are looking for. As an example, if you entered FOR SALE, it would automatically retrieve all messages with FOR SALE in the header. This will work for ALL aspects of the header. FROM, TO, DATE, SUBJECT and LOCATION. Even number of lines. All messages that meet these parameters are put in flagged memory and automatically retrieved. If there are no matches, it will tell you.

– T – Prints current Pacific coast time and date, and the length of time since you logged on.

– U – User modifiable functions. These are parameters which affect certain default conditions of the system. You modify them to your current needs.

A – Apple 40 mode. Toggles between 40 and 64 column message entry mode. Does not affect text output.

C – Case switch. Toggles between upper only and upper/ lower text OUTPUT. Lower case text is accepted during message entry and comments in either mode.

D – Duplex switch. Toggles between full (echo) and half (no echo) duplex modes. At this point in time, this function is only supported in Printer terminal mode (V) modifier.

L – Line feed switch. Turns linefeeds on or off. System default when you call, is on.

N – Nulls. Displays the current number of nulls in in effect, and allows you to modify them directly.

P – Prompt. Allows you to change the current system prompt, which is usually a (?) question mark. Here you can enter either the character you want the prompt to be, or the Ascii value of it. The prompt will stay defined as such through all system functions, until you change it again, or hang up. This feature can be used to good advantage with automatic upload or download programs. (automatic message entry, etc.)

V – Video/printer terminal mode toggle. In the video mode will accept data at full 300 baud. Recognizes ctrl-h underscore and rubout (asc08, 95 and 127 respectively) as backspace characters. In the printer mode, same characters are recognized, but during the backspacing addtional reverse slashes and the characters being backspaced over in reverse order will appear. This mode should not be used for automatic upload programs, as it is quite slow. Hope to change it soon. PAR – Parity. Allows you to modify the word length, type of parity, and number of stop bits employed. Displays a little chart with 8 positions. One of them will have a carot (^) under it, indicating the current system default at that time. Examples of numbers could be: 7E1 or 8N2 etc. 7E1 means 7 bit word, even parity and 1 stop bit. 8N2 would mean 8 bit word, No parity and 2 stop bits etc. Enter the position number 1-8 of the mode you need to use.

STAT – Displays current system status of all the modes covered by the U function, so you can see your current setup.

– X – eXpert user mode. Does away with the prompting at command level, the pausing between messages during a multiple retrieval and allows certain other priveledges.

– Z – Allows you to resume entering a message after you have aborted it. Let's say you were entering a message and realized you had forgotten something relevant to that message, and needed to reread an earlier message or article. You can abort the message, reread other messages or articles and then reenter your message with all data intact, and continue. You cannot, however, kill a message and then return.

– ? – Prints a list of all available commands available at your current mode of operation.

– * – Retrieve messages in flagged memory. This can be messages flagged during a scan or using the M or SR function.
You may pick up where you left off with this command, if you ended your retrieval for any reason. Using this command with scanning messages, (such as S;1000*) will clear the flagged memory completely for starting fresh.

> * * Message entry commands * *

– A – Abort message and return to command level. You may continue your message with the Z command if you have not tried to kill another message.

– C – Continue with message entry. Allows you to continue your message at whatever the next line in succession would be.

– D – Delete a line. Specify the number of the line you wish to delete. D;x & Dx are legal here. (x = line number)

– E – Edit or retype a message line. To replace the line, just enter the new line. Editing a line is accomplished by specifying a string you want to replace with what you want to replace it with, in this form: OLD/NEW with old and new string separated by a slash. You can also use three slashes as in the old editing routine: /OLD/NEW/. To remove a section of text type: OLD// or /OLD//. To insert text at the beginning of a line type: <this is new text. The left arrow means insert at the beginning. To append text at the end of a line type: >this is new text. The right arrow means append to the end. If you type a control-s (control-s only) as the first character of the line, the contents of the line will be automatically centered. If you are modifying an existing line and just type a control-s by itself, whatever is already on that line will be centered. Control-s as the first character of a line will also work during regular line entry (not just during edit). Ex and E;x (x = line number) are legal here.

– I – Insert a line. (Ix or I;x also legal) Allows you to insert a line directly BEFORE whatever line # you specify.

– S – Save the completed masterpiece to disk. You MUST use this command for your message to be saved!

– W – reWrite an old message. Using this command, you can kill an older message (with the correct password, of course) with the contents of it appearing in the message you are currently entering. The old message lines will be appended to your current position in the message. As an example, if you were at line 10 of a message, and wanted some data that was in an old message, use W and when it comes back, the contents of the message you killed will start at line 10. You can then edit or modify as required, then save it back out.

RCP/M

Sample RCP/M log on and menus are included in the previous chapter.

SECTION FOUR

DIRECTORIES

CHAPTER IX

Proper utilization of the following two lists of verified Bulletin Board System numbers will save you a lot of frustration and more than a little embarrassment.

As of this printing, of the approximate 1000 numbers collected, these 400-plus are the ones that continue to answer with a modem tone, signifying they are still operational.

Over half of the numbers we called were gone — usually disconnected. Some simply did not answer; possibly these were called at a 'wrong' hour. A small percentage were answered by irate, sleepy people ready to kill. (You would be too if you received telephone calls during all hours of the day and night, most of them mysterious hang-ups.)

The first list is a tabulation of numbers for all types of bulletin boards. It is set in numerical order by area code and phone number. Use it for quick reference to check for new numbers and bad (or discontinued) numbers.

The second is the BBS WORKBOOK itself. This contains the same numbers as the first in workbook form, allowing you to write in changes and additional comments. The BBS WORKBOOK numbers are sorted first by state, then by city, and then by type.

Your personal BBS WORKBOOK and LOGBOOKS, kept regularly updated, will prove indispensable, as inevitable changes (new boards, changed numbers, locations, options, etc.) occur.

CHAPTER IX

* QUICK REFERENCE LIST *

Computer Bulletin Boards sorted by area code and by number.

AREA CODE	PHONE NUMBER	TYPE OF BOARD	CITY
201	249-0691	RCP/M	Piscataway
201	272-1874	RCP/M	Cranford
201	291-8319	RCP/M	Atlantic Highlands
201	462-0435	DYM	Freehold
201	486-2956	FORUM-80	Union
201	543-6139	BBS	Mendham
201	584-9227	RCP/M	Flanders
201	747-7301	RCP/M	City
201	790-5910	BBS	Haledon
201	790-6795	BBS	Haledon
201	842-7644	CONN-80	Lindcroft
201	864-5345	ABBS	New York
201	891-9567	BBS	Wyckoff
201	994-9620	BBS	Livingston
202	276-8342	ARMUDIC	Washington
202	337-4694	BBS	Washington
202	635-5730	CBBS	Washington
203	227-4946	BULLET-80	Westport
203	372-1795	BULLET-80	Bridgeport
203	629-4375	BULLET-80	Westport
203	744-4644	BULLET-80	Danbury
203	746-5763	BBS	New Fairfield
203	888-7952	BULLET-80	Seymour
205	492-0373	BULLET-80	Gasden
206	256-6624	DYM	Vancouver
206	334-7394	BBS	Everett
206	357-7400	RCP/M	Olympia
206	458-3086	RCP/M	Olympia
206	546-6239	BBS	Seattle
206	762-5141	MINI-BIN	Seattle
206	763-8879	BBS	Seattle
206	883-0403	TSBBS	Redmond
207	839-2337	RCP/M	Gorham
209	227-2083	RCP/M	Fresno
212	245-4363	MSG-80	Manhattan
212	423-4623	BBS	Bayside
212	441-3755	BBS	Woodhaven
212	441-5719	BBS	Woodlawn
212	442-3874	BBS	Staten Island
212	541-5975	DYM	New York

AREA CODE	PHONE NUMBER	TYPE OF BOARD	CITY
212	626-0375	BBS	New York
212	740-5680	BULLET-80	New York
212	799-4649	TCBBS	New York
212	997-2488	PMS	New York
213	208-8255	BBS	West L.A.
213	276-0805	BBS	Beverly Hills
213	296-5927	RCP/M	West L.A.
213	306-1172	RCP/M	Venice
213	331-3574	PMS	Los Angeles
213	336-5535	BBS	Covina
213	346-1849	PMS	Woodland Hills
213	346-1861	PMS	Woodland Hills
213	360-5053	RCP/M	San Fernando
213	366-1238	BBS	San Fernando
213	368-4379	BBS	San Fernando
213	370-3293	RCP/M	Torrance
213	370-2887	KUG	Redondo
213	371-8825	BBS	Lawndale
213	388-5198	BBS	L.A.
213	390-3239	DYM	Mar Vista
213	394-5950	BBS	Santa Monica
213	428-5206	BBS	Long Beach
213	452-6111	DYM	Marina Del Rey
213	459-6400	BBS	Santa Monica
213	459-6400	ABBS	Pacific Palisades
213	470-4161	BBS	Westwood
213	473-2754	BBS	West L.A.
213	474-0270	SHOPPING	WEST L.A.
213	477-4605	BBS	WEST L.A.
213	516-9432	PAY DOWNLOAD	Gardena
213	537-3378	BBS	Compton
213	541-2503	BBS	Redondo Beach
213	577-9947	CBBS	Pasadena
213	649-1489	BBS	Culver City
213	653-6398	RCP/M	Hollywood
213	699-0775	BBS	Whittier
213	783-8373	ATARI	Van Nuys
213	790 3014	RCP/M	L.A. Area
213	796-6602	BBS	Pasadena
213	840-8252	DYM	Burbank
213	842-3322	BBS	Burbank
213	859-2735	BBS	Beverly Hills
213	881-6880	BBS	Tarzana
213	886-9221	BBS	Northridge
213	897-3012	BBS	San Fernando
213	902-1477	BBS	Van Nuys

AREA CODE	PHONE NUMBER	TYPE OF BOARD	CITY
213	902-1477	BBS	Van Nuys
213	944-5455	BBS	Whittier
213	973-2374	RCP/M	Hawthorne
213	980-5643	GAY	N. Hollywood
214	239-5842	NET-WORKS	Dallas
214	631-7747	X	Dallas
214	644-4781	NEW-WORKS	Dallas
214	769-3036	BBS	Hawkins
214	931 8274	RCP/M	Dallas
215	398 3937	RCP/M	Allentown
215	434-3998	BBS	Allentown
216	281-8820	DATACOM-80	Cleveland
216	486-4176	FORUM-80	Cleveland
216	645-0827	FORUM-80	Akron
216	724-2125	BBS	Akron
216	729-2769	BULLET-80	Chesterland
216	745-7855	ABBS	Akron
216	832-8392	PMS	Massillon
216	867-7463	PMS	Akron
216	875-4582	BBS	Louisville
216	932-9845	DYM	Cleveland
217	429-4738	NET-WORKS	Decatur
217	753-4309	MCMS	Springfield
301	251-6293	IBM PC	Gaithersburg
301	460-0538	IBM PC	Bethesda
301	465-3176	PMS	Ellicott City
301	565-9051	BBS	Forest Glen
301	587-2132	BBS	Baltimore
301	593-7033	BBS	Silver Spring
301	661 2175	RCP/M	Baltimore
301	948 5718	RCP/M	Gaithersburg
301	948-5717	CBBS	Gaithersburg
301	949-8848	IBM PC	Rockville
303	343-8401	HBBS	Denver
303	444-7231	RCP/M	Denver
303	499 9169	RCP/M	Boulder
303	690-4566	BBS	Denver
303	781 4937	RCP/M	Denver
303	985 1108	RCP/M	Denver
304	345-8280	NET-WORKS	Charleston
305	246-1111	BBS	Homestead
305	261-3639	ABBS	Miami
305	268-8356	BBS	Titusville
305	486-2983	ABBS	Ft. Lauderdale
305	525-1192	TRADE-80	Ft. Lauderdale

AREA CODE	PHONE NUMBER	TYPE OF BOARD	CITY
305	644-8327	BBS	Orlando
305	683-6044	BBS	W. Palm Beach
305	686-3695	BBS	W. Palm Beach
305	894-1886	CONN-80	Winter Garden
305	921-1127	BBS	Hollywood
305	948-8000	NET-WORKS	Miami
305	968-8653	GREEN MACH	Corsair WPB
307	637-6045	BBS	Cheyenne
309	342-7178	NET-WORKS	Galesburg
312	252 2136	RCP/M	Chicago
312	295-6926	PMS	Lake Forest
312	351-4374	MCMS	Schaumburg
312	352 5681	RCP/M	Chicago
312	359 8080	RCP/M	Chicago Area
312	359-9450	PBBS	Palatine
312	373-8057	PMS	Chicago
312	376-7598	IBM PC	Chicago
312	392-2403	ACS	Arlington Heights
312	397-0871	BBS	Chicago
312	397-8308	BBS	Palatine
312	420-7995	ABBS	Naperville
312	462-7560	MCMS	Wheaton
312	475-4884	ABBS	Chicago
312	545-8086	CBBS	Chicago
312	740-9128	HBBS	Round Lake
312	743-8176	BBS	Rogers Park
312	789-0499	ABBS	Oak Brook
312	789-3610	AMIS	Chicago
312	852-1305	CP/M	Downers Grove
312	897-9037	CBBS	Aurora
312	927-1020	BBS	Chicago
312	957-3924	BBS	Wenonah
312	957-3924	BBS	Chicago
312	963-5384	NET-WORKS	Chicago
312	964-6513	PMS	Downers Grove
313	335-8456	FORUM-80	Pontiac
313	348-4479	BBS	Detroit
313	455-4227	BBS	Detroit
313	465-9531	BBS	Mt. Clemens
313	483-0070	RCP/M	Schooner Cove
313	535-9186	RCP/M	Detroit
313	547-7903	BBS	Royal Oaks
313	559-5326	RCP/M	Southfield
313	683-5076	BULLET-80	Waterford
313	775-1649	BBS	Roseville
313	846 6127	RCP/M	Detroit

AREA CODE	PHONE NUMBER	TYPE OF BOARD	CITY
313	978-8087	AMIS	Sterling Heights
314	227-3258	RCP/M	Lethbridge
403	454 6093	RCP/M	Edmonton, ALB.
404	252-4146	IBM PC	Atlanta
404	252-9438	IBM PC	Atlanta
404	733-3461	ABBS	Atlanta
405	799-3393	CONN-80	Moore
406	443-2768	RCP/M	Helena Valley
408	255-8919	BULLET-80	Cupertino
408	298-6930	AMIS	San Jose
408	378 8733	RCP/M	Campbell
408	578 6185	RCP/M	San Jose
408	688-9629	PMS	Santa Cruz
408	867 1243	RCP/M	So. S.F. Bay
408	867-5486	BBS	So. S.F. Bay
409	846-2900	NET-WORKS	Bryan
412	822-7176	CBBS	Pittsburg
414	241-8364	CBBS	Thiensville
414	259-9475	BBS	Milwaukee
414	281-0545	TBBS	Milwaukee
414	355 8839	RCP/M	Milwaukee
414	554-9520	PET	Racine
414	563 9932	RCP/M	Ft. Atkinson
414	637-9990	ABBS	Racine
415	357-1130	CBBS	Berkeley
415	383 0473	RCP/M	S.F. Bay Area
415	452-0350	BBS	Oakland
415	462-7419	PMS	Pleasanton
415	467-2588	DYM	San Francisco
415	467-2588	MATCH	San Francisco
415	469-8111	ABBS X	San Francisco
415	538-3580	BBS	Hayward
415	552 9968	RCP/M	San Francisco
415	552-7671	BBS	San Francisco
415	595-0541	RCP/M	San Carlos
415	658-2919	CBBS	Berkeley
415	845-9462	IBM PC	Berkeley
415	851-3453	PMS	Portola Valley
415	895-0699	BBS	San Leandro
415	948-1474	BBS	So. S.F. Bay
415	991-4911	DYM	Daly City
416	223-2625	BBS	Toronto, Ont.
416	231-9538	RCP/M	Toronto, Ont.
416	423-3265	BBS	Toronto, Ont.
416	445-6696	NET-WORKS	Toronto, Ont.
416	447-8458	PMS	Toronto, Ont.

AREA CODE	PHONE NUMBER	TYPE OF BOARD	CITY
416	499-7023	IBM	Toronto, Ont.
416	624-5431	BBS	Ontario
419	867-9777	BBS	Toledo
501	646-0197	PMS	Ft. Smith
503	245-2536	PMS	Portland
503	535-6883	FORUM-80	Medford
503	621-3193	RCP/M	Burlington
504	273-3116	CBBS	Baton Rouge
504	889-2241	PMS	Metarie
504	926-0181	BBS	Baton Rouge
512	345-3752	BBS	Austin
512	385-1102	TBBS	Austin
512	442-1116	BBS	Austin
512	494-0285	BBS	San Antonio
513	489-0149	RCP/M	Cincinnatti
513	671-2753	PMS	Cincinnati
514	931-0458	ONLINE	Montreal, Que
516	293-5519	CONN-80	Massapqua
516	561-6590	CBBS	Long Island
516	588-5836	BBS	Centereach
516	627-9048	BBS	Manhasset
516	698-4008	ABBS	Long Island
516	924-8115	BBS	Yaphank, L.I.
517	339-3367	BBS	Lansing
518	346-3596	BBS	Albany
602	246-1432	BBS	Phoenix
602	274-5964	ACCESS	Phoenix
602	275-6644	BBS	Phoenix
602	293-4037	BBS	Tucson
602	458-3850	FORUM-80	Sierra Vista
602	746-3956	CBBS	Tucson
602	885-6775	BBS	Tucson
602	952-1382	BBS	Phoenix
602	952-2018	BBS	Phoenix
602	957-4428	ABBS	Phoenix
602	998-9411	BBS	Scotsdale
603	924-7920	BBS	Peterborough
604	437-7001	ABBS	Vancouver
604	937-0906	RCP/M	Frog Hollow
607	797-6416	SJBBS	Johnson City
608	262-4939	IBM PC	Madison
609	228-1149	ABBS	Turnersville
609	468-3844	RATS	Wenonah
609	468-5293	BBS	Wenonah
609	896-2436	BBS	Florenceville
612	533-1957	MCMS	Minneapolis

AREA CODE	PHONE NUMBER	TYPE OF BOARD	CITY
612	753-3082	MCMS	Minneapolis
612	929-6699	PMS	Minneapolis
612	929-8966	PMS	Minneapolis
614	475-9791	BBS	Gahana
614	837-3269	RCP/M	Pickerington
616	241-1971	AMIS	Grand Rapids
616	382-0101	ABBS	Kalamazoo
616	531-0890	HBBS	Grand Rapids
616	693-2648	BBS	Clarksville
617	266-7789	BULLET-80	Boston
617	334-6369	DYM	Lynnfield
617	353-9312	IBM PC	Boston
617	478-4164	RCP/M	Milford
617	683-2119	CBBS	Boston
617	689-7444	ACCESS-80	Andover
617	720-3600	BBS	Boston
617	891-1349	BBS	Waltham
617	966-0416	RCP/M	Bellingham
618	345-6638	NET-WORKS	St. Louis
619	256-3914	RCP/M	Barstow
619	271-8613	BBS	San Diego
619	283-3574	PMS	San Diego
619	434-4600	DYM	Carlsbad
619	443-6616	BBS	Lakeside
619	561-7271	ONLINE	Santee
619	561-7271	PMS	Lakeside
619	578-2646	PMS	San Diego
619	582-9557	PMS	San Diego
619	691-8367	BBS	San Diego
619	692-1961	ONLINE	San Diego
619	746-0667	PMS	Escondido
619	748-8746	DYM	Poway
702	826-7234	BBS	Reno
702	826-7277	BBS	Reno
702	870-9986	COMNET-80	Las Vegas
702	878-9106	PMS	Las Vegas
703	360-3812	BBS	Fairfax
703	360-5439	BBS	Alexandria
703	379-0303	BBS	Falls Church
703	425-9452	IBM	Fairfax
703	471-0610	ABBS	Herndon
703	536-3769	RCP/M	Arlington
703	560-0979	IBM PC	Annandale
703	560-7803	IBM PC	Vienna
703	670-5881	FORUM-80	Prince William
703	765-2161	BBS	Alexandria

AREA CODE	PHONE NUMBER	TYPE OF BOARD	CITY
703	978-7561	BBS	Fairfax
703	978-9592	IBM	Fairfax
704	365-4311	IBM PC	Charlotte
707	257-6502	RCP/M	Napa
707	422-7256	BBS	Fairfield
707	538-9124	BBS	Santa Rosa
713	331-2599	BULLET-80	Houston
713	333-2309	BBS	Houston
713	444-7041	BBS	Houston
713	455-9502	GABS	Houston
713	468-0174	BBS	Houston
713	469-8893	RCP/M	Houston
713	492-8700	BBS	Addicks Barker
713	556-1531	DYM	Houston
713	777-8608	BBS	Houston
713	871-8577	BBS	Houston
713	890-0910	IBM	Houston
713	933-7353	BBS	Houston
713	974-5258	BBS	Houston
714	354-8004	GREEN MACHINE	Riverside
714	359-3189	BBS	Riverside
714	524-1228	BBS	Fullerton
714	530-8226	BBS	Garden Grove
714	534-1547	BBS	Garden Grove
714	537-7913	BBS	Garden Grove
714	547-6220	BBS	Santa Ana
714	599-2109	BBS	Pomona
714	633-5240	BBS	Orange
714	772-8868	BBS	Anaheim
714	774-7860	RCP/M	Anaheim
714	877-2253	COMNET-80	Riverside
714	983-9923	BBS	Ontario
714	990-6747	BBS	Brea
715	352-2093	TBBS	Wausau
716	235-0512	BULLET-80	Rochester
716	425-1785	RCP/M	Upstate N.Y.
717	586-2112	BBS	Clarks Summit
801	776 5024	RCP/M	Roy
802	862-7023	ST80-CC	Burlington
803	279-5392	FORUM-80	Augusta
803	771-0922	BBS	Columbia
804	285-0041	BBS	Richmond
804	484-9636	BBS	Portsmouth
804	838-3973	DYM	Newport News
804	898-7493	RCP/M	Tidewater
805	492-5472	RCP/M	Thousand Oaks

AREA CODE	PHONE NUMBER	TYPE OF BOARD	CITY
805	527-9321	RCP/M	Simi Valley
805	682-7876	BBS	Santa Barbara
805	928-3254	BBS	Santa Maria
805	964-4115	BBS	Santa Barbara
806	792-0899	BULLET-80	Lubbock
808	487-2001	CONF-TREE	Honolulu
808	524-6612	NET-WORKS	Honolulu
812	858-5405	BBS	Newburgh
813	251-4095	BBS	Tampa
813	253-2393	OM-NET	Tampa
813	645-3669	BBS	Tampa
813	884-1506	BBS	Tampa
814	898-2952	TRADE-80	Erie
815	455-2406	ABBS	Crystal Lake
815	838-1020	MCMS	Lockport
816	252-0232	PMS	Kansas City
816	279-6859	CONN-80	St. Joseph
816	483-2526	NET-WORKS	Kansas City
816	861-7040	FORUM-80	Kansas City
816	931-9316	FORUM-80	Kansas City
817	767-5847	COMNET-80	Wichita Falls
901	276-8196	MEDICAL	Memphis
904	243-1257	ABBS	Destin
904	743-7050	PMS	Jacksonville
904	932-8271	NET-WORKS	Pensacola
907	243-0244	BBS	Anchorage
907	278-4223	BBS	Anchorage
907	344-5251	BBS	Anchorage
907	344-8558	PMS	Anchorage
907	349-6882	RCP/M	Anchorage
912	222-0863	DYM	Savannah
913	341-3502	PMS	Kansas City
913	341-3502	IBM PC	Mission
913	362-9583	RCP/M	Mission
913	432-5544	ONLINE	Mission
913	843-4259	RCP/M	Lawrence
914	679-6559	RCP/M	Upstate N.Y.
914	679-8734	RCP/M	Woodstock
914	782-7605	ST80-CC	Monroe
914	942-2638	RACS	Westchester
915	533-7039	ABBS	El Paso
915	565-9903	BULLET-80	El Paso
915	598-1668	RCP/M	El Paso
915	755-1000	FORUM-80	El Paso
919	274-3305	BBS	Greensboro
919	362-0676	DYM	Cary
919	692-7710	A.C.C.E.S.S.	Southern Pines

BBS WORKBOOK

ALASKA

907 243-0244	Anchorage	
BBS	ALPHA BOARD	
907 278-4223	Anchorage	
BBS	ABACUS NORTH	
907 344-5251	Anchorage	
BBS	CONFERENCE-TREE	
907 344-8558	Anchorage	
PMS	PMS	
907 349-6882	Anchorage	
RCP/M	ARCPM	
501 646-0197	Ft. Smith	
PMS	FT. SMITH COMP. CLUB	

ALABAMA

205 492-0373	Gasden
BULLET-80	

ARIZONA

602 957-4428	Phoenix
ABBS	DESERT TECHNOLOGY

BBS WORKBOOK

ARIZONA   cont'd.

_____

_____

_____

_____

_____

_____

_____

_____

_____

_____

_____

_____

_____

_____

_____

_____

_____

_____

_____

_____

_____

_____

_____

602 274-5964	Phoenix	
ACCESS	A-C-C-E-S-S	
602 246-1432	Phoenix	
BBS	APOLLO	
602 275-6644	Phoenix	
BBS	CALL-A-LAWYER	
602 952-1382	Phoenix	
BBS	BLAX-80	
602 952-2018	Phoenix	
BBS	OMEGA	
602 998-9411	Scottsdale JBS	
A-C-C-E-S-S		
602 458-3850	Sierra Vista	
FORUM-80		
602 293-4037	Tucson	
BBS	TUCSON DOWNLOAD	

BBS WORKBOOK

ARIZONA   cont'd.

_____

_____

_____

_____

_____

_____

602 885-6775   Tucson

BBS   HEATH

602 746-3956   Tucson

CBBS   TSG

CALIFORNIA

_____

_____

_____

_____

_____

_____

_____

_____

_____

_____

_____

714 772-8868   Anaheim

BBS   **IF**

714 774-7860   Anaheim

RCP/M   ANA-HUG

619 256 3914   Barstow

RCP/M   BARSTOW BOARD

617 966-0416   Bellingham

RCP/M   Bellingham RBBS

415 357-1130   Berkeley

CBBS   PROXIMA

415 658-2919   Berkeley

CBBS   CBBS/LAMBDA BERKELEY

BBS WORKBOOK

_____

_____

_____

_____

_____

_____

_____

_____

_____

_____

_____

_____

_____

_____

_____

_____

_____

415 845-9462	Berkeley	
IBM PC	BLUE BOSS	
213 276-0805	Beverly Hills	
BBS	THE INSANE ASYLUM	
213 859-2735	Beverly Hills	
BBS	THE PAWN SHOPPE	
714 990-6747	Brea	
BBS	BREA NET	
213 842-3322	Burbank	
BBS	MATCH MAKER #1	
213 840-8252	Burbank	
DYM	DYM #7	
408 378 8733	Campbell	
RCP/M	DBASE II	
619 434-4600	Carlsbad	
DYM	DYM #11	

BBS WORKBOOK

213 537-3378	Compton
BBS	ACCESS ONE
213 336-5535	Covina
BBS	NETWORKS GAMES
213 649-1489	Culver City
BBS	IBM-PC BBS
408 255-8919	Cupertino
BULLET-80	
415 991-4911	Daly City
DYM	DYM #17
619 746-0667	Escondido
PMS	
707 422-7256	Fairfield
BBS	RBBS/RCPM
209 227-2083	Fresno
RCP/M	OxGate-005 Micro Fone

BBS WORKBOOK

_____

_____

_____

_____

_____

_____

_____

_____

_____

_____

_____

_____

_____

_____

_____

_____

_____

_____

_____

714 524-1228	Fullerton	
BBS	RACS V	
714 530-8226	Garden Grove	
BBS	OCTUG OR. COUNTY	
714 534-1547	Garden Grove	
BBS	GFRN DATA EXC. 2	
714 537-7913	Garden Grove	
BBS	OR. CTY DATA EXCH	
213 516-9432	Gardena	
PAY DOWNLOAD	TSC DOWNLOAD	
213 973-2374	Hawthorne	
RCP/M	Hawthorne RBBS	
415 538-3580	Hayward	
BBS	CONFERENCE-TREE #3	
213 653-6398	Hollywood	
RCP/M	HOLLYWOOD RCP/M	

BBS WORKBOOK

_____

_____

_____

_____

_____

_____

_____

_____

_____

_____

_____

_____

_____

_____

_____

_____

_____

213 388-5198   L.A.

BBS   MAGNETIC FANTASIES

213 790 3014   L.A. Area

RCP/M   LA CANADA RBBS

619 443-6616   Lakeside

BBS   DATEL AFTER HOURS

619 561-7271   Lakeside

PMS

213 371-8825   Lawndale

BBS   COMPUTERLAND

213 428-5206   Long Beach

BBS   DRAGON'S LAIR

213 331-3574   Los Angeles

PMS   PEOPLES MSG. SYS.

213 390-3239   Mar Vista

DYM   DYM#19

BBS WORKBOOK

213 452-6111	Marina Del Rey
DYM	DYM #36
213 980-5643	N. Hollywood
GAY	ORACLE
707 257 6502	Napa
RCP/M	NAPA VL. RBBS/RCPM
213 886-9221	Northridge
BBS	HW COMPUTERS
415 452-0350	Oakland
BBS	SUNRISE OMEGA-80
714 983-9923	Ontario
BBS	CMPTRS. FOR CHRIST
714 633-5240	Orange
BBS	NOCC BULLETIN SYSTEM
213 459-6400	Pacific Palisades
ABBS	ABBS

BBS WORKBOOK

CALIFORNIA   cont'd.

_____

_____

_____

_____

_____

_____

_____

_____

_____

_____

_____

_____

_____

_____

_____

_____

_____

213 796-6602	Pasadena	
BBS	PIRATE GALLEY	
213 577-9947	Pasadena	
CBBS		
415 462-7419	Pleasanton	
PMS	PMS PLEASANTON	
714 599-2109	Pomona	
BBS	SAN DIMAS RCP/M	
415 851-3453	Portola Valley	
PMS		
619 748-8746	Poway	
DYM	DYM #33	
213 370-2887	Redondo	
KUG	WORDMOVERS	
213 541-2503	Redondo Beach	
BBS	GFRN DATA EXCH. 1	

BBS WORKBOOK

_____

_____

_____

_____

_____

_____

_____

_____

_____

_____

_____

_____

_____

_____

_____

_____

_____

714 359-3189   Riverside

BBS   BULLET-80

714 877-2253   Riverside

COMNET-80

714 354-8004   Riverside

GREEN MACHINE

415 383 0473   S.F. Bay Area

RCP/M   RBBS OF MARIN CNTY.

415 595 0541   San Carlos

RCP/M   DATATECH NETWORK

619 271-8613   San Diego

BBS   PMS DATEL

619 691-8367   San Diego

BBS   CVBBS

619 692-1961   San Diego

ONLINE   SABA

BBS WORKBOOK

_____

_____

_____

_____

_____

_____

_____

_____

_____

_____

_____

_____

_____

_____

_____

_____

_____

_____

_____

619 283-3574   San Diego

PMS   GAMEBOARD

619 578-2646   San Diego

PMS   KID'S MESSAGE SYSTEM

619 582-9557   San Diego

PMS   COMPUTER MERCHANT

213 366-1238   San Fernando

BBS   MOG-UR'S BBS

213 368-4379   San Fernando

BBS   MIDNITE MADNESS

213 897-3012   San Fernando

BBS   DATA CONNECTION

213 360-5053   San Fernando

RCP/M   GRANADA ENG. GROUP

415 469-8111   San Francisco

ABBSX   SOUTH OF MARKET

BBS WORKBOOK

_____

_____

_____

_____

_____

_____

_____

_____

_____

_____

_____

_____

_____

_____

_____

415 552-7671	San Francisco	
BBS	S.F.DRUMMER MAG.	
415 467-2588	San Francisco	
DYM	DYM #10	
415 467-2588	San Francisco	
MATCH	S.F.MATCHMAKER	
415 552 9968	San Francisco	
RCP/M	RICH & FAMOUS	
408 298-6930	San Jose	
AMIS	IBBBS	
408 578 6185	San Jose	
RCP/M	SKYHOUSE SYSTEMS	
415 895 0699	San Leandro	
BBS	SYSTEM/80	
714 547-6220	Santa Ana	
BBS	VERGA-80	

BBS WORKBOOK

_____

_____

_____

_____

_____

_____

_____

_____

_____

_____

_____

_____

_____

_____

_____

_____

_____

_____

805 682-7876	Santa Barbara
BBS	REMOTE NORTHSTAR
805 964-4115	Santa Barbara
BBS	REMOTE NORTHSTAR
408 688-9629	Santa Cruz
PMS	
805 928-3254	Santa Maria
BBS	PHREQUE-OUT
213 394-5950	Santa Monica
BBS	BR'S BBS
213 459-6400	Santa Monica
BBS	ABBS
707 538-9124	Santa Rosa
BBS	STTRS-80
619 561-7271	Santee
ONLINE	

BBS WORKBOOK

_____

_____

_____

_____

_____

_____

_____

_____

_____

_____

_____

_____

_____

_____

_____

_____

_____

_____

805 527-9321	Simi Valley	
RCP/M	CP/M-NET	
408 867-5486	So. S.F. Bay	
BBS		
415 948-1474	So. S.F. Bay	
BBS	PCNET BBS	
408 867 1243	So. S.F. Bay	
RCP/M	OXGATE-001	
213 881-6880	Tarzana	
BBS	NOVATION	
805 492-5472	Thousand Oaks	
RCP/M	RCP/M	
213 370 3293	Torrance	
RCP/M	S. BAY RCPM/RBBS	
213 783-8373	Van Nuys	
ATARI	LAACE BBS	

BBS WORKBOOK

_____

_____

_____

_____

_____

_____

_____

_____

_____

_____

_____

_____

_____

_____

213 902-1477	Van Nuys
BBS	Electric Line Connect.
213 306 1172	Venice
RCP/M	PATVAC
213 477-4605	WEST L.A.
BBS	INTERFACE BB
213 474-0270	WEST L.A.
SHOPPING	BUY-PHONE
213 208-8255	West L.A.
BBS	FUTURE SHIELD
213 473-2754	West L.A.
BBS	SOFTWORX
213 296-5927	West L.A.
RCP/M	SOFTWAIRE CENTRE
213 470-4161	Westwood
BBS	H.W. COMPUTERS

BBS WORKBOOK

CALIFORNIA   cont'd. ─────

213 699-0775	Whittier
BBS	BGGS
213 944-5455	Whittier
BBS	THE APPLE BOARD
213 346-1849	Woodland Hills
PMS	O. A. C. PMS
213 346-1861	Woodland Hills
PMS	PEOPLE'S MSG. SYS.

COLORADO ─────

303 499-9169	Boulder
RCP/M	BOULDER RCPM
303 690-4566	Denver
BBS	CONNECTION-80
303 343-8401	Denver
HBBS	AURORA-NET
303 444-7231	Denver
RCP/M	REMOTE NORTHSTAR

BBS WORKBOOK

COLORADO cont'd.

303 781 4937	Denver
RCP/M	DENVER CUG-NODE
303 985 1108	Denver
RCP/M	Lakewood RCPM/RBBS

CONNECTICUT

203 372-1795	Bridgeport
BULLET-80	
203 744-4644	Danbury
BULLET-80	
203 746-5763	New Fairfield
BBS	TELCOM 7
203 888-7952	Seymour
BULLET-80	HEADQUARTERS
203 629-4375	Westport
BULLET-80	
203 227-4946	Westport
BULLET-80	

BBS WORKBOOK

DISTRICT OF COLUMBIA

_____
_____
_____

_____
_____
_____

_____
_____
_____

FLORIDA

_____
_____
_____

_____
_____
_____

_____
_____
_____

_____
_____
_____

202 276-8342	Washington
ARMUDIC	ATARI USERS GROUP
202 337-4694	Washington
BBS	THE PROGRAM STORE
202 635-5730	Washington
CBBS	CUA TIMESHARING
305 968-8653	Corsair WPB
GREEN MACH	
904 243-1257	Destin
ABBS	FT WALTON BEACH
305 486-2983	Ft. Lauderdale
ABBS	BYTE SHOP
305 525-1192	Ft. Lauderdale
TRADE-80	
305 921-1127	Hollywood
BBS	BIG FOOT

BBS WORKBOOK

_____

_____

_____

_____

_____

_____

_____

_____

_____

_____

_____

_____

_____

_____

_____

_____

_____

_____

_____

_____

_____

_____

305 246-1111	Homestead
BBS	LIVING VIDEOTEXT
904 743-7050	Jacksonville
PMS	
305 261-3639	Miami
ABS	BYTE SHOP
305 948-8000	Miami
NET-WORKS	BIG APPLE
305 644-8327	Orlando
BBS	CONNECTION-80
904 932-8271	Pensacola
NET-WORKS	BEACH BBS
813 251-4095	Tampa
BBS	ALPHA
813 645-3669	Tampa
BBS	APOLLO'S CHARIOT

BBS WORKBOOK

_____
_____
_____

_____
_____
_____

_____
_____
_____

_____
_____
_____

_____
_____
_____

_____
_____
_____

_____
_____
_____

813 884-1506   Tampa

BBS   MICRO INFORMER

813 253-2393   Tampa

OM-NET

305 268-8356   Titusville

BBS   SPACECOAST

305 848-3802   W. Palm Beach

ABBS

305 683-6044   W. Palm Beach

BBS   INFOEX-80

305 686-3695   W. Palm Beach

BBS   MICRO-80

305 686-4862   W. Palm Beach

BBS   THE NOTEBOOK

305 894-1886   Winter Garden

CONN-80

BBS WORKBOOK

GEORGIA

_____
_____
_____

_____
_____
_____

_____
_____
_____

_____
_____
_____

_____
_____
_____

| **404 733-3461** | Atlanta |
| ABBS | AGS |

| **404 252-4146** | Atlanta |
| IBM PC | HOSTCOMM |

| **404 252-9438** | Atlanta |
| IBM PC | |

| **803 279-5392** | Augusta |
| FORUM-80 | |

| **912 222-0863** | Savannah |
| DYM | DYM #3 |

HAWAII

_____
_____
_____

_____
_____
_____

| **808 487-2001** | Honolulu |
| CONF-TREE | COMPUTERLAND |

| **808 524-6612** | Honolulu |
| NET-WORKS | COMPUTER MARKET |

IOWA

_____
_____
_____

| **319 353-6528** | Iowa City |
| ABBS | APPLE-MED |

BBS WORKBOOK

_____
_____
_____

_____
_____
_____

_____
_____
_____

_____
_____
_____

_____
_____
_____

_____
_____
_____

312 392-2403	Arlington Heights
ACS	

312 897-9037	Aurora
CBBS	Aurora Peripherals

312 475-4884	Chicago
ABBS	GAMEMASTER

312 789-3610	Chicago
AMIS	

312 397-0871	Chicago
BBS	PET BBS, COMMODORE

312 622-4442	Chicago
BBS	MCMS MESSAGE-82

312 927-1020	Chicago
BBS	MCMS CAMS

312 957-3924	Chicago
BBS	C.M.M.S.

BBS WORKBOOK

312 545-8086	Chicago
CBBS	CBBS #1
312 647-7636	Chicago
CP/M	
312 376-7598	Chicago
IBM PC	
312 963-5384	Chicago
NET-WORKS	APPLE NET
312 373-8057	Chicago
PMS	PMS
312 252 2136	Chicago
RCP/M	LOGAN SQUARE
312 352 5681	Chicago
RCP/M	CHICAGO C-NODE
312 359 8080	Chicago Area
RCP/M	PALATINE

BBS WORKBOOK

_____

_____

_____

_____

_____

_____

_____

_____

_____

_____

_____

_____

_____

_____

_____

_____

_____

_____

815 455-2406	Crystal Lake
ABBS	NESSY FLYNN's BBS
217 429-4738	Decatur
NET-WORKS	C.A.M.S.
312 852-1305	Downers Grove
CP/M	
312 964-6513	Downers Grove
PMS	DOWNERS GRV./SRT
309 342-7178	Galesburg
NET-WORKS	MAGIE
312 598-4861	Hickory Hills
BBS	CALL-80
312 295-6926	Lake Forest
PMS	NIAUG
815 838-1020	Lockport
MCMS	J.A.M.S.

BBS WORKBOOK

ILLINOIS cont'd. ————————————

312 420-7995	Naperville	
ABBS	Illini Microcomputer	
312 789-0499	Oak Brook	
ABBS	AIMS	
312 397-8308	Palatine	
BBS	OS-9 6809 BS	
312 359-9450	Palatine	
PBBS	CO-OP Computer Serv.	
312 743-8176	Rogers Park	
BBS	MARS/RP	
312 740-9128	Round Lake	
HBBS	L.A.M.S.	
312 351-4374	Schaumburg	
MCMS	WACO HOT LINE	
217 753-4309	Springfield	
MCMS	WORD EXCHANGE	

BBS WORKBOOK

ILLINOIS cont'd.

_____

_____

_____

_____

_____

_____

INDIANA

_____

_____

_____

_____

_____

_____

_____

_____

_____

_____

_____

KANSAS

_____

_____

_____

_____

_____

312 957-3924	Wenonah
BBS	RATS
312 462-7560	Wheaton
MCMS	P.C.M.S.
317 326-4152	Greenfield
NET-WORKS	
317 255-5435	Indianapolis
BBS	PET BBS AVC CMLN.
317 787-5486	Indianapolis
PMS	
812 858-5405 M	Newburgh
BBS	Net-Works Base Unit
913 843 4259	Lawrence
RCP/M	ALPHANET
913 362 9583	Mission
RCP/M	MISSION

BBS WORKBOOK

KANSAS   cont'd.

316 663-3600	Hutchinson
BBS	
913 341-3502	Mission
IBM PC	
913 432-5544	Mission
ONLINE	Dickenson's Movie Guide
316 682-2113	Wichita
FORUM-80	
316 682-9093	Wichita
RCP/M	Wichita RBBS/RCPM

LOUISIANNA

504 926-0181	Baton Rouge
BBS	Baton Rouge Data System
504 273-3116	Baton Rouge
CBBS	
504 889-2241	Metarie
PMS	

BBS WORKBOOK

MASSACHUSETTS

617 689-7444	Andover
ACCESS-80	
617 720-3600	Boston
BBS	PIRATE'S HARBOR
617 266-7789	Boston
BULLET-80	
617 683-2119	Boston
CBBS	LAWRENCE GN HOSP.
617 353-9312	Boston
IBM PC	COMPUTER SOCIETY
617 334-6369	Lynnfield
DYM	DYM #18
617 891-1349	Waltham
BBS	PIRATE'S CHEST

MARYLAND

301 587-2132	Baltimore
BBS	COMPUTER AGE

BBS WORKBOOK

MARYLAND cont'd. ————————————

	301 661 2175	Baltimore
	RCP/M	BHEC
	301 460-0538	Bethesda
	IBM PC	
	301 465-3176	Ellicott City
	PMS	PMS
	301 565-9051	Forest Glen
	BBS	TECH-LINK
	301 948-5717	Gaithersburg
	CBBS	CPEUG/ICST
	301 251-6293	Gaithersburg
	IBM PC	
	301 948 5718	Gaithersburg
	RCP/M	MICROCMPTR. ELEC.
	301 949-8848	Rockville
	IBM PC	

BBS WORKBOOK

MARYLAND cont'd. ─────────

_____

_____

_____

301 593-7033	Silver Spring
BBS	HEX

MAINE ─────────

_____

_____

_____

_____

_____

_____

207 839-2337	Gorham
RCP/M	PROGRAMMER'S ANON.
617 478-4164	Milford
RCP/M	MILFORD RCP/M

MICHIGAN ─────────

_____

_____

_____

_____

_____

_____

_____

_____

_____

616 693-2648	Clarksville
BBS	RS-CPM
313 455-4227	Detroit
BBS	GBBS
313 348-4479	Detroit
BBS	WESTSIDE DOWNLOAD
313 535 9186	Detroit
RCP/M	MINICBBS
313 846 6127	Detroit
RCP/M	TECHNICAL CBBS

BBS WORKBOOK

_____
_____
_____

_____
_____
_____

_____
_____

_____
_____

_____
_____

_____
_____

_____
_____

_____
_____
_____

_____
_____
_____

616 241-1971	Grand Rapids
AMIS	G.R.A.S.S.
616 531-0890	Grand Rapids
HBBS	HEATH/ZENITH
616 382-0101	Kalamazoo
ABBS	COMPUTER ROOM
517 339-3367	Lansing
BBS	CONNECTION-80
313 465-9531	Mt. Clemens
BBS	FORUM-80
313 335-8456	Pontiac
FORUM-80	
313 775-1649	Roseville
BBS	TWILIGHT PHONE
313 547-7903	Royal Oaks
BBS	TREASURE ISLAND

BBS WORKBOOK

MICHIGAN   cont'd. ————————————————————

_____

_____

_____

_____

_____

_____

_____

_____

_____

_____

_____

313 483-0070	Schooner Cove
RCP/M	Schooner Cove RCP/M
313 559 5326	Southfield
RCP/M	SOUTHFIELD
313 978-8087	Sterling Heights
AMIS	A.R.C.A.D.E.
313 683-5076	Waterford
BULLET-80	

MINNESOTA ————————————————————

_____

_____

_____

_____

_____

_____

_____

_____

_____

612 533-1957	Minneapolis
MCMS	NC SOFTWARE
612 753-3082	Minneapolis
MCMS	GOLIATH
612 929-6699	Minneapolis
PMS	PMS
612 929-8966	Minneapolis
PMS	

BBS WORKBOOK

_____

_____

_____

_____

_____

_____

_____

_____

_____

_____

_____

_____

_____

_____

_____

_____

314 532-4652	Chesterfield
BBS	FORTH DIMENSION
816 861-7040	Kansas City
FORUM-80	
816 931-9316	Kansas City
FORUM-80	Market Commodities
816 483-2526	Kansas City
NET-WORKS	ABC
816 252-0232	Kansas City
PMS	APPLE BITS
913 341-3502	Kansas City
MJPMS	APPLE BITS
816 279-6859	St. Joseph
CONN-80	
618 345-6638	St. Louis
NET-WORKS	WARLOCK'S CASTLE

BBS WORKBOOK

314 227 3258	St. Louis
RCP/M	OXGATE-009
314 227-4312	St. Louis
X	MIDWEST

MONTANA

406 443-2768	Helena Valley
RCP/M	Helena Val. RBBS/RCPM

NEBRASKA

402 339-7809	Omaha
ABBS	ABBS
402 292-9598	Omaha
BBS	OACPM
402 571-8942	Omaha
DYM	DYM #23

NORTH CAROLINA

919 362-0676	Cary
DYM	DYM #20
704 365-4311	Charlotte
IBM PC	

BBS WORKBOOK

NORTH CAROLINA cont'd.

_____

_____

_____

_____

_____

919 274-3305	Greensboro
BBS	Small Time User Group

919 692-7710	Southern Pines
A.C.C.E.S.S.	

NEW HAMPSHIRE

_____

_____

_____

603 924-7920	Peterborough
BBS	CONNECTION-80

NEW JERSEY

_____

_____

_____

_____

_____

_____

_____

_____

_____

_____

_____

_____

201 747-7301	
RCP/M	P. Bogdanovich's

201 291-8319	Atlantic Highlands
RCP/M	KUG NJ1 BBS

201 272-1874	Cranford
RCP/M	RIBBS of Cranford

201 584 9227	Flanders
RCP/M	FLANDERS

609 896-2436	Florenceville
BBS	DELTA CONNECTION

BBS WORKBOOK

_____

201 462-0435	Freehold
DYM	DYM #21
201 790-5910	Haledon
BBS	APHRODITE EAST
201 790-6795	Haledon
BBS	PHOTO-80
201 842-7644	Lindcroft
CONN-80	
201 543-6139	Mendham
BBS	PIRATE'S I
201 249 0691	Piscataway
RCP/M	CP/M-NET ™ EAST
609 228-1149	Turnersville
ABBS	
201 486-2956	Union
FORUM-80	

BBS WORKBOOK

NEW JERSEY   cont'd.

_____

_____

_____

_____

_____

_____

609 468-5293	Wenonah
BBS	STARS
609 468-3844	Wenonah
RATS	

NEVADA

_____

_____

_____

_____

_____

_____

_____

702 870-9986	Las Vegas
COMNET-80	
702 878-9106	Las Vegas
PMS	CENTURY 23
702 826-7234	Reno
BBS	SIGN-ON
702 826-7277	Reno
BBS	SIGN-ON

NEW YORK

_____

_____

_____

_____

518 346-3596	Albany
BBS	CAPITAL CITY BBS
212 423-4623	Bayside
BBS	COCO'S

BBS WORKBOOK

_____

_____

_____

_____

_____

_____

_____

_____

_____

_____

_____

_____

_____

_____

_____

_____

_____

_____

_____

_____

516 588-5836   Centereach

BBS   CONNECTION-80

---

607 797-6416   Johnson City

SJBBS

---

201 994-9620   Livingston

BBS   THE BARN

---

516 698-4008   Long Island

ABBS   PIRATES COVE

---

516 561-6590   Long Island

CBBS   LICA LIMBS

---

516 627-9048   Manhasset

BBS   PIRATE'S LODGE

---

212 245-4363   Manhattan

MSG-80

---

516 293-5519   Massapqua

CONN-80

BBS WORKBOOK

914 782-7605	Monroe	
ST80-CC	MONROE CAMERA SHOP	
201 864-5345	New York	
ABBS	ABBS NEW YORK	
212 626-0375	New York	
BBS	NYBBLES-80	
212 740-5680	New York	
BULLET-80		
212 541-5975	New York	
DYM		
212 997-2488	New York	
PMS	MCGRAW-HILL BOOKS	
212 799-4649	New York	
TCBBS	W.E.B.B.	
716 235-0512	Rochester	
BULLET-80		

BBS WORKBOOK

_____

_____

_____

_____

_____

_____

_____

_____

_____

_____

_____

_____

_____

_____

_____

_____

_____

_____

315 337-7720   Rome

GREEN MACHINE

---

212 442-3874   Staten Island

BBS   SISTER

---

716 425 1785   Upstate N.Y.

RCP/M   ROCHESTER

---

914 679 6559   Upstate N.Y.

RCP/M   BEARSVILLE TOWN

---

914 942-2638   Westchester

RACS

---

212 441-3755   Woodhaven

BBS   CONNECTION-80

---

212 441-5719   Woodlawn

BBS

---

914 679-8734   Woodstock

RCP/M   Woodstock RCP/M

BBS WORKBOOK

NEW YORK   cont'd.

_____
_____
_____

_____
_____

OHIO
_____
_____

_____
_____

_____
_____

_____
_____

_____
_____

201 891-9567	Wyckoff
BBS	THE SANCTUARY
516 924-8115	Yaphank, L.I.
BBS	SCCA
216 745-7855	Akron
ABBS	AKRON DIGITAL GROUP
216 724-2125	Akron
BBS	INFOEX-80
216 645-0827	Akron
FORUM-80	N. OHIO BUS. USERS
216 867-7463	Akron
PMS	RAUG
216 729-2769	Chesterland
BULLET-80	
513 671-2753	Cincinnati
PMS	

BBS WORKBOOK

_____

_____

_____

_____

_____

_____

_____

_____

_____

_____

_____

_____

_____

_____

513 489-0149	Cincinnatti	
RCP/M	Cincinnatti RBBS	
216 281-8820	Cleveland	
DATACOM-80		
216 932-9845	Cleveland	
DYM	DYM #34	
216 486-4176	Cleveland	
FORUM-80		
614 475-9791	Gahana	
BBS	APPLE CRACKERS	
216 875-4582	Louisville	
BBS	MICRO-COM	
216 832-8392	Massillon	
PMS	PEOPLE'S MSG. SERV.	
614 837 3269	Pickerington	
RCP/M	PICKERINGTON RBBS	

BBS WORKBOOK

OHIO cont'd. ——————————————

419 867-9777	Toledo
BBS	Toledo Apple Users Gr.

OKLAHOMA ——————————————

405 799-3393	Moore
CONN-80	

OREGON ——————————————

503 621-3193	Burlington
RCP/M	Chuck Forsberg's RCPM
503 535-6883	Medford
FORUM-80	
503 245-2536	Portland
PMS	

PENNSYLVANIA ——————————————

215 434-3998	Allentown
BBS	HERMES-80
215 398 3937	Allentown
RCP/M	ALLENTOWN RBBS
717 586-2112	Clarks Summit
BBS	BULLET-80

BBS WORKBOOK

PENNSYLVANIA   cont'd.

_____

_____

_____

814 898-2952   Erie

TRADE-80

_____

_____

_____

412 822-7176   Pittsburg

CBBS   PACC

SOUTH CAROLINA

_____

_____

803 771-0922   Columbia

BBS   COMPUSYSTEMS

TENNESSEE

_____

_____

901 276-8196   Memphis

MEDICAL   FORUM-80

TEXAS

_____

_____

_____

713 492-8700   Addicks Barker

BBS   WEEKENDER

_____

_____

_____

512 345-3752   Austin

BBS

_____

_____

_____

512 442-1116   Austin

BBS   AUSTIN PARTY BOARD

_____

_____

_____

512 385-1102   Austin

TBBS

BBS WORKBOOK

_____

_____

_____

_____

_____

_____

_____

_____

_____

_____

_____

_____

_____

_____

_____

_____

_____

_____

409 846-2900   Bryan

NET-WORKS   COLLEGE STATION

214 239-5842   Dallas

NET-WORKS   ECLECTIC COMP. SYS.

214 644-4781   Dallas

NEW-WORKS   APPLE SHACK

214 931 8274   Dallas

RCP/M   DALLAS RCP/M CBBS

214 631-7747   Dallas

X   THE PULSE

915 533-7039   El Paso

ABBS

915 565-9903   El Paso

BULLET-80

915 755-1000   El Paso

FORUM-80

BBS WORKBOOK

_____

_____

_____

_____

_____

_____

_____

_____

_____

_____

_____

_____

_____

_____

_____

_____

_____

_____

_____

_____

_____

915 598 1668	El Paso
RCP/M	EL PASO RCP/M
214 769-3036	Hawkins
BBS	BULLET-80
713 333-2309	Houston
BBS	DARK REALM
713 444-7041	Houston
BBS	COMPUQUE-80
713 468-0174	Houston
BBS	JOLLY ROGER #1
713 777-8608	Houston
BBS	SHADOW WORLD
713 871-8577	Houston
BBS	MINES OF MORIA
713 933-7353	Houston
BBS	ZACHARY NET

BBS WORKBOOK

_____

_____

_____

_____

_____

_____

_____

_____

_____

_____

_____

_____

_____

_____

_____

_____

_____

_____

713 974-5258	Houston	
BBS	PIRATE'S PALACE	
713 331-2599	Houston	
BULLET-80		
713 556-1531	Houston	
DYM	DYM #12	
713 455-9502	Houston	
GABS	THE GREAT APPLE	
713 890-0910	Houston	
IBM	HOSTCOMM	
713 469 8893	Houston	
RCP/M	SATSUMA RCP/M	
806 792-0899	Lubbock	
BULLET-80		
512 494-0285	San Antonio	
BBS	SATUG BBS	

BBS WORKBOOK

TEXAS   cont'd.

_____   **817 767-5847**   Wichita Falls

_____

_____   COMNET-80

UTAH

_____   **801 776 5024**   Roy

_____

_____   RCP/M   N. UTAH CP/M USR GRP

VIRGINIA

_____   **703 360-5439**   Alexandria

_____

_____   BBS   FUTURE TECH

_____   **703 765-2161**   Alexandria

_____

_____   BBS   SWITCHBOARD

_____   **703 560-0979**   Annandale

_____

_____   IBM PC

_____   **703 536-3769**   Arlington

_____

_____   RCP/M   Arlington RCPM/DBBS

_____   **703 360-3812**   Fairfax

_____

_____   BBS   C-HUG BBS

_____   **703 978-7561**   Fairfax

_____

_____   BBS   FAMILY HISTORIANS

BBS WORKBOOK

VIRGINIA   cont'd. ————————————

_____

_____

_____

_____

_____

_____

_____

_____

_____

_____

_____

_____

_____

_____

_____

_____

_____

703 425-9452	Fairfax
IBM	HOSTCOMM
703 978-9592	Fairfax
IBM	HOSTCOMM
703 379-0303	Falls Church
BBS	Potomac Micro Magic
703 471-0610	Herndon
ABBS	SOFTWARE SORCERY
804 838-3973	Newport News
DYM	DYM #32
804 484-9636	Portsmouth
BBS	TALK-80 ROBB
703 670-5881	Prince William
FORUM-80	
804 285-0041	Richmond
BBS	SKELETON ISLAND

BBS WORKBOOK

VIRGINIA cont'd.

804 898 7493	Tidewater
RCP/M	OXGATE-007 GRAFTON
703 560-7803	Vienna
IBM PC	

VERMONT

802 862-7023	Burlington
ST80-CC	LANCE MICKLUS INC.

WASHINGTON

206 334-7394	Everett
BBS	MSG-80
206 357-7400	Olympia
RCP/M	OLYMPIA RCPM
206 458 3086	Olympia
RCP/M	YELM RBBS & CP/M
206 883-0403	Redmond
TSBBS	TIMEX SINCLAIR
206 546-6239	Seattle
BBS	AMSAT BBS

BBS WORKBOOK

206 763-8879	Seattle
BBS	SEACOMM-80
206 762-5141	Seattle
MINI-BIN	MINI-BIN
206 256-6624	Vancouver
DYM	DYM #16

WISCONSIN

414 563 9932	Ft. Atkinson
RCP/M	FORT FONE FILE
608 262-4939	Madison
IBM PC	
414 259-9475	Milwaukee
BBS	BIG TOP GAMES SYS.
414 355 8839	Milwaukee
RCP/M	BEER CITY BBS
414 281-0545	Milwaukee
TBBS	CANOPUS

BBS WORKBOOK

WISCONSIN cont'd.

_____

_____

_____

_____

_____

_____

_____

_____

_____

WEST VIRGINIA

_____

_____

WYOMING

_____

_____

CANADA

_____

_____

_____

_____

414 637-9990   Racine

ABBS   Colortron Computer

414 554-9520   Racine

PET   BBS S.E.W.P.U.G.

414 241-8364   Thiensville

CBBS

715 352-2093   Wausau

TBBS   Central WI Comp. Con.

304 345-8280   Charleston

NET-WORKS   CHARLESTON NETWORK

307 637-6045   Cheyenne

BBS   PET BBS

604 437-7001   Vancouver

ABBS

403 454 6093   Edmonton, ALB.

RCP/M   EDMONTON RCPM

BBS WORKBOOK

CANADA   cont'd.

604 937 0906	Frog Hollow
RCP/M	FROG HOLLOW CBBS
403 320-6923	Lethbridge
BBS	LETHBRIDGE GMNG SYS
514 931-0458	Montreal, Que
ONLINE	COMPUTERLAND
416 624-5431	Ontario
BBS	PET BBS PSI WORDPRO
416 223-2625	Toronto, Ont.
BBS	PET BBS TPUG
416 423-3265	Toronto, Ont.
BBS	THE BULL
416 499-7023	Toronto, Ont.
IBM	HOSTCOMM
416 445-6696	Toronto, Ont.
NET-WORKS	

BBS WORKBOOK

CANADA   cont'd. ─────────────────────

416 447-8458	Toronto, Ont.
PMS	LOGIC INC.

416 231 9538	Toronto
RCP/M	Toronto Ontario RCP/M

BBS WORKBOOK

SECTION FIVE

ON-LINE LOGBOOKS

CHAPTER X

CHAPTER XI

CHAPTER X

ON-LINE BBS LOGBOOK

* Personal Equipment Log * On-Line Logbook

PERSONAL EQUIPMENT LOG

	TYPE	SERIAL NUMBER
Computer 1		
Computer 2		
Computer 3		
Modem		
Modem		
Printer		
Printer		

NOTES : _____

_____

_____

_____

_____

CHAPTER XI

ELECTRONIC MAIL ADDRESS BOOK

NAME	Electronic/MAIL ADDRESS CODE	SYSTEM NAME	PHONE NUMBER	COMMENTS

ELECTRONIC MAIL ADDRESS BOOK

NAME	Electronic/MAIL ADDRESS CODE	SYSTEM NAME	PHONE NUMBER	COMMENTS

ELECTRONIC MAIL ADDRESS BOOK

NAME	Electronic/MAIL ADDRESS CODE	SYSTEM NAME	PHONE NUMBER	COMMENTS

ONLINE BBS LOGBOOK

NUMBER CALLED	DATE	TIME LOG-ON	LOG-OFF	SYSTEM NAME	TYPE	PASSWORD	ADDRESS CODE	SYSOP	HOURS	ON-LINE ACTIVITIES, COMMENTS

ONLINE BBS LOGBOOK

NUMBER CALLED	DATE	TIME LOG-ON	LOG-OFF	SYSTEM NAME	TYPE	PASSWORD	ADDRESS CODE	SYSOP	HOURS	ON-LINE ACTIVITIES, COMMENTS

ONLINE BBS LOGBOOK

NUMBER CALLED	DATE	TIME LOG-ON	LOG-OFF	SYSTEM NAME	TYPE	PASSWORD	ADDRESS CODE	SYSOP	HOURS	ON-LINE ACTIVITIES, COMMENTS

ONLINE BBS LOGBOOK

NUMBER CALLED	DATE	TIME LOG-ON	LOG-OFF	SYSTEM NAME	TYPE	PASSWORD	ADDRESS CODE	SYSOP	HOURS	ON-LINE ACTIVITIES, COMMENTS

ONLINE BBS LOGBOOK

NUMBER CALLED	DATE	TIME LOG-ON	LOG-OFF	SYSTEM NAME	TYPE	PASSWORD	ADDRESS CODE	SYSOP	HOURS	ON-LINE ACTIVITIES, COMMENTS

SECTION SIX

RESOURCES

CHAPTER XII

CHAPTER XIII

CHAPTER XIV

NOTES:

CHAPTER XII

* Addresses Of Modem Manufacturers and Software Vendors
* Buyer's Guide To Modems * Buyer's Guide To Communication Software

MODEM MANUFACTURERS AND COMMUNICATIONS SOFTWARE VENDORS

ADVENTURE INTERNATIONAL
P.O. Box 3435
Longwood, FL 32750
(305) 830-8194

ALPHA SOFTWARE CORP.
2 New England Executive Park
Burlington, MA 01813

APPLE COMPUTER INC.
20525 Mariani Ave.
Cupertino, CA 95014
(800) 538-9696

ATARI
1265 Borregas Avenue
Sunnyvale, CA 94086
(408) 745-2000

BIZCOMP CORP.
P.O.Box 7498
Menlo Park, CA 94026
(408) 745-1616

COMMODORE COMPUTERS
487 Devon Park Drive
Wayne, PA 19087
(215) 687-9750

GENERAL DATACOM
INDUSTRIES INC.
One Kennedy Avenue
Danbury, CT 06810
(203) 797-0711

HAYES MICROCOMPUTER
PRODUCTS
5835 Peachtree Corners East
Norcross, GA 30092
(404) 449-8792

INCOMM
115 North Wolf Road
Wheeling, IL 60090
(312) 459-8881

LEXICON CORP.
1541 N.W. 65th Ave.
Fort Lauderdale, FL 33313
(305) 792-4400

LIFEBOAT ASSOCIATES
1651 Third Ave.
New York, NY 10028
(212) 860-0300

LINK SYSTEMS
1640 19th St.
Santa Monica, CA 90404
(213) 453-1851

MFJ ENTERPRISES INC.
P.O. Box 494
Mississippi State, MS 39762
(800) 647-1800

MICROCOM
1400A Providence Highway
Norwood, MA 02062
(617) 762-9310

MICROSTUF INC.
1900 Leland Dr.
Marietta, GA 30067
(404) 952-0267

MICRO-SYSTEMS SOFTWARE INC.
4301-18 Oak Circle
Boca Raton, FL 33431
(405) 983-3390

MOUNTAIN COMPUTER INC.
300 El Pueblo Road
Scotts Valley, CA 95066
(408) 438-6650

MULTI TECH SYSTEMS INC.
82 2nd Ave. S.E.
New Brighton, MN 55112
(612) 631-3550

NOVATION
18664 Oxnard St.
Tarzana, CA 91346
(800) 423-5419

OSBORNE COMPUTER CORP.
26500 Corperate Ave.
Hayward, CA 94545
(415) 887-8080

PMMI COMMUNICATIONS
5201 Leesburg Pike, Suite 604
Falls Church, VA 22041
(703) 379-9660

RACAL VADIC
222 Caspian Drive
Sunnyvale, CA 94086
(408) 744-0810

RADIO SHACK-TANDY CORP.
1 Tandy Center
Fort Worth, TX 76102
(817) 390-3011

RIXON INC.
2120 Industrial Parkway
Silver Spring, MD 20904
(301) 622-2121

SOUTHEASTERN SOFTWARE
7743 Briarwood Dr.
New Orleans, LA 70128
(504) 246-8438

SOUTHWESTERN DATA SYSTEMS
P.O. Box 582
Santee, CA 92071
(714) 562-3670

SSM MICROCOMPUTER PRODUCTS
2190 Paragon Drive
San Jose, CA 95131
(800) 227-2400

UNIVERSAL DATA SYSTEMS
5000 Bradford Drive
Huntsville, AL 35805
(205) 837-810029

U.S. ROBOTICS INC.
1035 West Lake St.
Chicago, IL 80607
(312) 733-0497

VISIONARY ELECTRONICS INC.
141 Parker Ave.
San Francisco, CA 94118
(415) 751-8811

MODEM CHART

MANUFACTURER	MODEL	COMPUTER / TYPE	DIR.	ACOUS	110	300	1200	103	113	212	212A	202	Full	Half	A/A	ONLY ORIG.	ONLY ANS.	ANS. ORIG.	SOFTWARE INCLUDED	SPECIAL FEATURES	PRICE
ATARI																					
	Communicator II Kit	Atari	yes			yes		yes					yes	yes		yes			yes	auto logon	$280
	(includes modem)																			auto-dial	
BIZCOMP CORP.																					
	Model 1080	Commodore	yes			yes		yes	yes				yes			yes					$139
		Apple, Atari																	scroll. buffer		
COMMODORE																					
	Vic Modem	Vic-20	yes		yes	yes		yes					yes	yes				yes	yes		$110
	Commodore-64																				
	AutoVic	same	yes		yes	yes		yes					yes	yes	yes			yes	yes	auto-dial	$180
																				self test	
DATEC																					
	Model 30	RS-232 Port		yes	yes	yes		yes	yes				yes	yes		yes					$225
	Model 33	RS-232 Port	yes		yes	yes		yes	yes						yes			yes			$219
	Model 212	RS-232 Port	yes		yes	yes	yes	yes		yes			yes	yes	yes					self test	$595
GENERAL DATACOM INDUSTRIES																					
	GDC 103J-L	RS-232 Port	yes		yes	yes		yes	yes				yes	yes		yes	yes			self test	$200
	GDC 103J-M	RS-232 Port	yes		yes	yes		yes	yes				yes		yes	yes	yes			self test	$250
HAYES MICROCOMPUTER PRODUCTS																					
	Micromodem 100	S-100 Bus	yes		yes	yes		yes					yes	yes	yes			yes	yes	auto-dial	$399
	Micromodem II	Apple II, II	yes		yes	yes		yes					yes	yes	yes			yes	yes	auto-dial	$409
	Smartmodem 300	RS-232 Port	yes		yes	yes		yes					yes	yes	yes			yes		auto dial	$289
																				auto-redial	
																				programmable	
	Smartmodem 1200	RS-232 Port	yes		yes	yes	yes	yes			yes		yes	yes	yes			yes		self test same	$699
INCOMM																					
	Auto Dial A212A	RS-232 Port	yes			yes	yes	yes			yes		yes	yes	yes			yes		auto dial	?
																				self test	
																				blt.in speak.	
	M1200	RS-232 Port	yes				yes	yes			yes		yes		yes	yes	yes	yes		self test	?
LEXICON CORP.																					
	Lex-11	RS-232 Port	yes		yes	yes		103A					yes	yes	yes	yes	yes	yes		self test	$160

MODEM CHART

MANUFACTURER / MODEL	COMPUTER / TYPE	PHONE CONNECT DIR.	PHONE CONNECT ACOUS	BAUD RATE 110	300	1200	BELL STANDARD 103	113	212	212A	202	DUPLEX Full	Half	A/A	MODE ONLY ORIG.	ONLY ANS.	ANS ORIG.	SOFTWARE INCLUDED	SPECIAL FEATURES	PRICE
MFJ ENTERPRISES INC																				
MFJ-1232	RS-232 Port		yes	yes	yes		yes					yes	yes				yes	optional	cassette I/O	$130
	Apple II game port w/ optional software																		battery	
MULTI-TECH SYS INC.																				
Modem II	Apple II, II+	yes		yes	yes	yes	yes	yes				yes	yes	yes			yes	firmware	auto-dial w/storage progrmmble.	$399
Multi-Modem II	same	yes		yes	yes	yes	yes	yes	yes			yes	yes	yes			yes	same	same	$799
NOVATION INC.																				
CAT	R-232 Port		yes		yes		yes					yes	yes	yes		yes				auto-dial auto-redial self test	$189
D-CAT	RS-232 Port	yes			yes		yes	yes				yes	yes			yes				hold funct. auto-dial self test	$199
J-CAT	RS-232 Port	yes			yes		yes					yes	yes	yes			yes		auto-search self test very small	$149
Auto-CAT	RS-232 Port	yes			yes		yes	yes				yes	yes	yes		yes			auto dial auto-redial self test	$249
212 Auto-CAT	RS-232 Port	yes			yes	yes	yes	yes		yes		yes	yes	yes		yes			auto-dial self test aut. discnnt.	$695
Apple-CAT II	Apple II, II+	yes		yes	yes	yes	yes	yes		yes	yes	yes	yes	yes				yes	auto-dial auto-redial expandable	$389
Smart-CAT 103	RS-232 Port	yes		yes	yes	yes	yes					yes	yes	yes				yes	auto-dial	$249
Smart-CAT 103/212	RS-232 Port	yes		yes	yes	yes				yes		yes		yes			yes	yes	21commands same	$595
OSBORNE																				
COMM-PAC	Osborne I	yes			yes		yes					yes		yes			yes	yes	auto-dial auto-redial	$265

MODEM CHART

MANUFACTURER / MODEL	COMPUTER / TYPE	DIR.	ACOUS	110	300	1200	103	113	212	212A	202	Full	Half	A/A	ONLY ORIG.	ONLY ANS.	ANS ORIG.	SOFTWARE INCLUDED	SPECIAL FEATURES	PRICE
OMNITECH DATA																				
770			yes		yes		yes					yes					yes			$179
9123AD	RS-232 Port	yes			yes	yes	yes	yes									yes		auto-switch of voice to data	$225
913BO	RS-232 Port	yes			yes		yes					yes		yes					auto-dial auto-redial	$499
9212AO	RS-232 Port	yes			yes	yes	yes	yes		yes		yes		yes			yes		auto-dial	$724
PMMI COMMUNICATIONS INC																				
MM-103	S-100 Bus	yes		yes	yes		yes					yes		yes			yes	yes	auto-dial programmble. 5 yr. warrnty.	$360
RACAL VADIC																				
VA 212LC	RS-232 Port	yes			yes	yes	yes			yes		yes		yes			yes		auto dial self test	$495
VA 212PA	RS-232 Port	yes			yes	yes	yes			yes							yes		auto dial 15 numbers progrmmble.	$795
RACAL VADIC																				
VA 212PA	RS-232 Port	yes			yes	yes	yes			yes							yes		auto dial 15 numbers progrmmble. 16 key cntrl. pnl., slf. test	$795
VA 355	RS-232 Port	yes			yes		yes	yes				yes					yes		self test	$375
RADIO SHACK																				
TRS-80 Modem I	TRS-80																			
w/RS-232 port	yes			yes	yes						yes					yes		$149		
RIXON INC.																				
R103J	RS-232 Port	yes		yes	yes		yes	yes				yes		yes			yes		talk/data switch	$199
PC 1200	RS-232 Port	yes		yes	yes	yes	yes	yes	yes			yes		yes			yes		same	$499
R212A	RS-232 Port	yes		yes	yes	yes	yes	yes	yes			yes		yes			yes		same built-in auto-dialr.	$895

MODEM CHART

Manufacturer / Model	Computer / Type	DIR.	ACOUS	110	300	1200	103	113	212	212A	202	Full	Half	A/A	Only Orig.	Only Ans.	Ans. Orig.	Software Included	Special Features	Price
SSM MICROCOMPUTER PRODUCTS																				
Apple Modem Card	Apple II	yes		yes	yes		yes	yes				yes	yes	yes		yes		yes		$299
Modem 1200	RS-232 Port	yes			yes	yes	yes			yes		yes	yes	yes				yes	auto-dial / self test	$695
UNIVERSAL DATA SYSTEMS																				
UDS 202LP	RS-232 Port	yes		yes	yes						yes	yes					yes	talk/data switch / tele. line powered	$245
UDS 212A	RS-232 Port	yes		yes	yes	yes	yes	yes		yes		yes		yes					self test	$695
UDS 212A/D	RS-232 Port	yes		yes	yes	yes	yes	yes		yes		yes		yes					self test / 5 number auto-dial	$795
U.S. ROBOTICS INC																				
Phone Link	RS-232 Port		yes	yes	yes		yes	yes				yes	yes				yes	yes	self test	$149
Little Link	RS-232 Port	yes		yes	yes		yes	yes				yes	yes				yes			$139
Micro Link 1200	RS-232 Port	yes				yes			yes	yes			yes	yes				yes	self test	$449
Auto Dial 212A	RS-232 Port	yes		yes	yes	yes	yes		yes	yes		yes	yes	yes			yes	yes	auto-dial / auto-redial / self test	$599
VISIONARY ELECTRONICS INC.																				
MODEL 100	RS-232 Port	yes			yes		yes	yes				yes		yes			yes	yes	2K to 24K memory / 8085 procssr. to 8K / control program / clock/clndr. / auto-send/receive / fully progr.	$595 / $760

SOFTWARE CHART

COMPANY Product	COMPUTER SYSTEM SUPPORTED	AUTO LOG—ON	BAUD RATE SUPPORTED			MENU DRIVEN	VERIFY MODE	EDIT MODE	MAX FILE	PRICE
			110	300	1200				(SIZE)	
ADVENTURE INTER.										
Combat	TRS-80 I, III-32K	?	yes	yes	yes					
APPLE I – 48K; ATARI-24K										
ALPHA SOFTWARE CORP										
The Apple-IBM	IBM PC-64K,1disk,RS232			yes					disk	$195
Connection	Apple II-64K, 1 disk									
	Micromodem II									
APPLE COMPUTER										
Comm-pac	Apple II+ - 48K,									
	Micromodem II	yes		yes		yes		yes	140K	$85
Micro Courier III	Apple III-128K or 256K	yes	yes	yes	yes	yes	yes	screen	disk	?
	Hayes Smartmodem									
Access III	Apple III-128K SOS	yes	yes	yes	yes	yes	yes	full	disk	$150
	all RS-232 modems									
ATARI										
Telelink II cart.	Atari	yes		yes	yes					Included
COMMODORE										
Victerm 40	Vic-20		yes	yes		yes	yes	yes	disk	$40
HAYES MICROCOMPUTER										
PRODUCTS										
Smartcom II (IBM)	IBM PC-96K,1 disk									
	Hayes Smartmodem 300/1200	yes	yes	yes	yes	yes	yes	yes	disk	$119
Smartcom II	Xerox 820-II, 2-8"drives,									
(Xerox 820-II)	Smartmodem 300 or 1200	yes	yes	yes	yes	yes	yes	yes	disk	$119
Hayes Terminal	Apple II-48K, 1 drive		yes	yes	yes	yes	yes	yes	disk	$99
Program	DOS 3.3, Pascal, CP/M									
Micromodem II										
LIFEBOAT ASSOCIATES										
ASCOM	CP/M 80 & 86; MSDOS	yes	yes	yes	yes		yes		disk	
BSTAM	CP/M 80 & 86		yes	yes	yes		yes		disk	$150
BSTMS	CP/M	yes	yes	yes	yes	yes			disk	$150
RTBE-80	CP/M		yes	yes	yes	yes			disk	
eZ MAIL	CP/M		yes	yes	yes	yes		yes	disk	$149
LINK SYSTEMS										
DataLink	Apple II-64K, Apple Pascal	yes	yes	yes	yes	yes	yes		disk	$100
	Micromodem II									
	Novation Apple Cat									
DataLine	Apple III-128K	yes	yes	yes	yes	yes	yes		disk	$150
	Micromodem II									
MFJ ENTERPRISES INC.										
MFJ-1231	Apple II +		yes	yes		yes	yes	yes	disk	$40
MICROCOM										
MICRO/Terminal	Apple II, III; IBM PC	yes		yes	yes	yes		full	disk	$85-100
MICRO/Courier	Apple II, III; IBM PC			yes		yes	yes	some	disk	$150
	TRS-80 Model III									

SOFTWARE CHART

COMPANY Product	COMPUTER SYSTEM SUPPORTED	AUTO LOG-ON	BAUD RATE SUPPORTED			MENU DRIVEN	VERIFY MODE	EDIT MODE	MAX FILE	PRICE
			110	300	1200				(SIZE)	
MICROSTUF INC.										
Crosstalk	CP/M, CP/M 86, MP/M, DOS	yes	yes	yes	yes		yes	?	disk	$195
	Min 32K; Bell 103/212A									
	compatible modems									
MICRO-SYSTEMS										
SOFTWARE INC.										
MicroTerm	Zenith Z-100	yes	yes	yes	yes	yes	yes		disk	$80 up
	IBM PC; TRS-80									
MOUNTAIN										
COMPUTER INC.										
Communications	Apple II,III; Atari 800;		yes	yes	yes	yes			disk	$75
Software System	IBM PC; TRS-80 II,III									
Level I	Osborne									
Level II	same		?	yes	?	yes	yes		?	$150
NOVATION										
Com-Ware II	Apple II, II +		yes	yes	yes	yes			?	
SOUTHEASTERN										
SOFTWARE										
Data Capture/pc	IBM PC-64K		yes	yes	yes	yes		line	disk	$120
Data Capture 4.0	Apple II w/Apple	yes		yes		yes		line	18K	$65
	communications card									
Data Capture 4.0/80	Apple II; Micromodem II	yes	yes	yes	yes	yes		some	20K	$90
	Prometheus Versacard									
	Super Serial Card									
SOUTHWESTERN										
DATA SYSTEMS										
Ascii Express-	Apple II, II + - 48K	yes	yes	yes	yes	yes	yes	full	disk	$130
The Professional										
P Term-	Same							Pascal		
The Professional	Pascal	yes	yes	yes	yes	yes	yes	Editor	disk	$130
Z Term-	Same	yes	yes	yes	yes	yes	yes	CP/M	disk	$150
The Professional	CP/M							Editor		
SSM MICROCOMPUTER										
PRODUCTS INC.										
Transend 1	Apple II, III		yes	yes	yes	yes	yes	yes	disk	$89
	Novation Apple Cat									
	Ven-Tel,Prentice,UDS									
Transcend 2	same	yes	yes	yes	yes	yes	yes		disk	$149
Transcend 3	same	yes	yes	yes	yes	yes	yes	yes	disk	$275
SUPERSOFT										
Term II	CP/M	yes		yes	yes	yes	yes	yes	disk	$200
U.S. ROBOTICS										
Compak	CP/M		yes	yes	yes	yes	yes		disk	$50
WESTICO										
ASCOM	IBM PC	yes	yes	yes	yes	yes	yes	yes	disk	$175

NOTES:

CHAPTER XIII

RESOURCES

* Commercial Online Databases * Users Groups * Public Domain Software * Computer Bulletin Board Programs * Directories And Newsletters * Books * Magazine Articles *

* * * COMMERCIAL ONLINE DATABASES * * *

BRS

Bibliographic Retrieval Services
1200 Route 7
Latham, NY 12110
(800) 833-4707

CompuServe

CompuServe Information Service
5000 Arlington Centre Blvd.
P.O. Box 20201
Columbus, Ohio 43220
(800) 848-8119

DIALOG

Dialog Information Services Inc.
3460 Hillview Ave.
Palo Alto, CA 94304
(800) 277-1927
(800) 982-5838 (CA)

Dow Jones (DJNS)

Dow Jones and Company Inc.
Dow Jones News/Retrieval Service
P.O. Box 300
Princeton, NJ 08540
(800) 257-5114

DELPHI

General Videotext Corporation
3 Blackstone St.
Cambridge, MA 02139
(617) 491-3393
(800) 544-4005

NewsNet

NewsNet
945 Haverford Road
Bryn Mawr, PA 19010
(215) 527-8030
(800) 345-1301

NYTIS

New York Times Information Service
1719A – Route 10
Parsippany, NJ 07054
(201) 539-5850

ORBIT

ORBIT Information Retrieval System
SDC Search Service
2500 Colorado Avenue
Santa Monica, CA 90406

SOURCE

SOURCE Telecomputing Corporation
1616 Anderson Road
McLean, VA 22102
(800) 336-3366

* * * USERS GROUPS * * *

APPLE

The International Apple Corps
908 George St.
Santa Clara, CA 95050
(408) 727-7652

The Big Apple Users Group
P.O. 490
Bowling Green Station
New York, NY 10274

Northern Illinois Apple Users Group
1271 West Dundee Rd.
Buffalo Grove, IL 60090

Boston Apple Users Group
3 Center Plaza
Boston, MA 02108

ATARI

Atari Computer Users Group Support
Program
P.O. 50047
San Jose, CA 95150

COMMODORE

Commodore
Computer Systems Group
487 Devon Park Dr.
Wayne, PA 19087
(215) 687-9750

HEATH/ZENITH

HUG (Heath Users Group)
Hilltop Rd.
St. Joseph, MI 49085

HEWLETT-PACKARD

Users' Library
1000 Northeast Circle Blvd.
Corvallis, OR 97330
(503) 757-2000

NORTH STAR

Marketing Communications
North Star Computers Inc.
14440 Catalina St.
San Leandro, CA 94577
(415) 357-8500

OSBORNE

Glenn Evans
184 Downey St.
San Francisco, CA 94117

Osborne Users Group
P.O. 190
Oceanside, NY 11572

Denver Osborne Users Group
P.O. 521
Kittredge, CO 80457

First Osborne Users Group
P.O. 11683-A
Palo Alto, CA 94306

Osborne Computer Corporation
26538 Danti Court
Hayward, CA 94545
(415) 887-8080

RADIO SHACK

International Color Computer Club
2101 E. Main St.
Henderson, TX 75652

Tucson Color Computer Users Group
Box 15186
Tucson, AZ 85708

Columbus TRS-80 Color Computer
Users Group
527 Malvern Dr.
Painesville, OH 44077

* * * USER'S GROUPS * * *

RADIO SHACK (cont'd.)

TRS-80 Users Group Inc.
P.O. 400472
Dallas, TX 75240

South Bay TRS-80 Users Group
P.O. 60116
Sunnyvale, CA 94088

Tampa Bay TRS-80 Users Group
1721 Greenlee Dr.
Clearwater, FL 33515

TRS-80 Users Group of Atlanta
1637 Columbia Dr.
Decatur, GA 30034

TEXAS INSTRUMENTS

TI 99/4 Users Group
P.O. 267
Leesburg, VA 22075

T. I. (cont'd.)

MSP 99 User Group
P.O. 12351
St. Paul, MN 55112

St. Louis 99ers
3429 Pesta Lozzi
St. Louis, MO 63118

TIMEX/SINCLAIR

ZX Timex Users Group
Box 2443
Titusville, FL 33742

Sinclair Users Network
2170 Oak Brook Circle
Palatine, IL 60074

ZX81/TS1000 Users
P.O. 2411
Vista, CA

* * * PUBLIC DOMAIN SOFTWARE * * *

Listed below are computer user's groups and help groups that specialize in the distribution of public domain software. Check to see if they have a version of modem7 already configured for your computer. They have a large selection of public domain software and documentation on file which they provide at very low cost.

CPMUG

CP/M Users Group
1651 Third Ave.
New York, NY 10028

NYACC

New York Amateur Computer Club
P.O. Box 106
Church St. Station
New York, New York 10008

SIG/M

Special Interest Group/Microcomputers
SIG/M User's Group
Amateur Computer Club of New Jersey, Inc.
P.O. Box 97
Islen , NJ 08830

* * * COMPUTER BULLETIN BOARD PROGRAMS * * *

In order to set up your own bulletin board, you will need a special bulletin board program. Many of the programs available are listed below in the following format:

NAME OF PROGRAM	COMPUTER PROGRAM RUNS ON
Contact	Address
Telephone	
Cost of Program	

ABBS 4.0 Software Sorcery	**APPLE II** 7927 Jones Branch Dr., + 400 McLean, VA 22102
ACCESS Information Intelligence Inc. (602) 996-2283 $750	**APPLE II +** P.O. Box 31098 Phoenix, AZ 85046
AMIS GRAFex Company (408) 996-2689 $10	**ATARI 800** Box 1558 Cupertino, CA 95015
Bullet-80 Computer Services of Danbury $150	**TRS-80 model I/III** P.O. Box 993 Danbury, CT 06810
CBBS Randy Suess (312) 545-8086 $50	**CP/M computers** 5219 W. Warwick Chicago, IL 60641
Hostcomm N.F. Systems Ltd. (404) 252-4146 $170	**IBM PC** P.O. Box 76363 Atlanta, GA 30358
Net-Norks Nick Naimo 47630 $89.95	**APPLE II** 4877 Martin Rd. Newburgh, IN 47630
NorthStar BBS The MicroStuf Company Decatur, GA 30033	**NORTH STAR** P.O. Box 33337
PC-BBS George Peck $75.00	**IBM PC** 5900 Canterbury Drive #A-219 Culver City, CA 90230
People's Message System Bill Blue Lakeside, CA 92040	**APPLE II** P.O. Box 1318
MOUSE-NET Lance Micklus $299	**TRS-80 Model I/III** 217 South Union Street Burlington, VT
ST80-X10, ST80-PB, ST80-CC Small Bus. Systems Group Westford, MA 01866	**TRS-80 Model I/III** 6 Carlisle Road
Message-80 Microperipheral Corporation Mercer Island, WA 98040	**TRS-80 Model I/III** P.O. Box 529
Great Apple Bulletin Board GABBS Inc. Houston, TX 77229	**APPLE II +** P.O. Box 24343

* * * DIRECTORIES AND NEWSLETTERS * * *

COMPUTER-READABLE DATABASES: A DIRECTORY AND DATA SOURCEBOOK

Knowledge Industry Publications, Inc.
701 Winchester Ave.
White Plains, Ny 10604

DATAPRO DIRECTORY OF ON-LINE SERVICES

Datapro Research Corporation
1805 Underwood Boulevard
Dalran, NJ 08075

DIAL-OUT (newsletter)

175 5th. Ave. Suite 3371
New York, NY 10010

DIRECTORY OF ON-LINE DATABASES

Cuadra Associates, Inc.
2001 Wilshire Blvd. Suite 305
Santa Monica, CA 90403

ELECTRONIC MAIL & MESSAGE SYSTEMS
(newsletter)

International Resource Development, Inc.
30 High Street
Norwalk, CT 06851

ENCYCLOPEDIA OF INFORMATION SYSTEMS AND SERVICES

Gale Research Company
Book Tower
Detroit, MI 48226

ON-LINE COMPUTER TELEPHONE DIRECTORY

OLCTD
P.O. Box 10005
Kansas City, MO 64111

* * * BOOKS * * *

Glossbrenner, Alfred
The Complete Handbook of Personal Computer Communications:
Everything You Need to Know to Go Online with the World
St. Martin's Press, New York, 1983
[excellent overview of commercial databases]

Shapiro, Neil L.
The Small Computer Connection: Telecommunications
for the Home & Office
Micro Text/McGraw-Hill, New York, 1983

Sippl, Charles J.
Microcomputer Dictionary
Radio Shack, U.S.A., 1981

Tydeman, J., H. Lipinski, R. Adler, M. Nyhan, L. Zwimpfer
Teletext and Videotex in the United States: Market Potential,
Technology, Public Policy Issues
McGraw-Hill, New York, 1982
[social implications of the computer revolution]

* * * Magazine Articles * * *

Bronson, Ben, and Kelly Smith and Keith Peterson
"Using RCPM Systems Effectively"
Microsystems
Vol. 4, no. 4, 1983, pp. 42-44

Derfler, Frank J., J2.
"Dial-Up Apple: A Communications Sampler"
In Cider
Vol. 1, no. 6, 1983, pp. 74-92

Edwards, John
"Buyer's Guide to On-Line Information Services"
Desktop Computing
Vol. 3, no. 5, 1983, pp. 16-20

Edwards, John
"Where to Find User Groups"
Popular Computing
Vol. 2, No. 11, 1983, pp. 174-178

Ferrand. Peter, and John Davidson
"Worlds of Information"
In Cider
Vol. 1, no. 6, 1983, pp. 80-84

Friedman, Herb
"Modems"
Radio Electronics
Vol. 54, no. 4, 1983, pp. 85-89

Gerber, Carol Houze
"Networks: Personal Links in the Electronic Universe"
Today
June, 1983, pp. 12-18

Gerber, Carol Houze
"Speedy Information: Electronic Messaging and Computer Originated Mail"
Today
June, 1983, pp. 21-23

Hewen, Larry M., & Duane Saylor
"Telecomputing . . . the Next Great Wave"
Desktop Computing
Vol. 3, no. 5, 1983, pp. 34-36

James, Ralph L.
"A Terminal Program for the TRS-80 Model III"
Byte
Vol. 8, no. 2, 1983, pp. 458-467

* * * Magazine Articles * * *

Magnin, Ed
"Telecommunications Adviser"
In Cider
Vol. 1, no.6, 1983, pp. 66-70

Metzger, Elizabeth
"The Helping Hands Of Computer Clubs"
Personal Computing
Vol. 7, no.3, 1983, pp. 142-147

Miller, Darby
"Videotex: Science Fiction or Reality?"
Byte
Vol. 8, no.7, 1983, pp. 42-56

Newell, Jud, and Kim Levitt
"List of RCPM Systems"
User's Guide to CP/M Systems & Software
Vol. 1, no. 3, 1983, pp. 24-28

Rosen, Bob
"Portable Communications"
PCM
Vol. 1, no. 1, 1983, p.13

Sheldon, Ken
"Dial 'O' . . . But Not for O'Malley"
Desktop Computing
Vol. 3, no. 5, 1983, pp. 27-29

Smith, Kelly
"CP/M '83 Report"
"User's Guide to CP/M Systems & Software"
Vol. 1, no. 3, 1983, pp. 30-37

Smith, Kelly, & Tony Bove
"Downloading from RCPM Systems"
User's Guide to CP/M Systems & Software
Vol. 1, no. 3, 1983, pp. 13-23

The', Lee
"Data Communications: A Buyer's Guide To Modems And Software"
Personal Computing
Vol. 7, no. 3, 1983, pp. 96-128

Yuen, Matthew
"Some Computers Shoot Electronic Arrows"
Softalk
February, 1983, pp. 164-68

NOTES:

CHAPTER XIV

GLOSSARY

ACOUSTIC TYPE MODEM — To use this type of modem, you simply set the phone receiver into two fitted rubber cups. Acoustic modems require no plugs or adapters. They can be used with any standard telephone. This type of modem is susceptible to high room noise. If you use an acoustic modem for long periods of time, you might want to replace the normal carbon-granule microphone in your telephone with a condenser microphone. The carbon granules have a tendency to compact after hours of modem use, which decreases the reliability of communications.

AUTO-ANSWER — Modems with this feature can automatically answer the phone and establish contact with the computer that is calling.

AUTO-DIAL — Modems or communications programs with this feature automatically dial your most frequently used telephone numbers.

AUTO-REDIAL — Modems with this feature can automatically redial busy numbers. This is great when you are trying to reach an extremely busy board.

BAUD — refers to the speed at which information is transmitted. Baud rate is roughly equivilent to words per minute. 300 baud is the most common speed found on BBS's, with 1200 baud now becoming more popular. At 1200 baud, information is transfered four times faster than at 300 baud. Saving time saves money.

BBS — Acronym for (B)ulletin (B)oard (S)ystem

COMMUNICATIONS CARD — Some computers require additional hardware in order to connect a modem. (. . . but you said the PRINTER was the last thing it would ever need . . .)

COMPATIBILITY — There are several different modem standards. They all achieve the same end by different means. For two systems to communicate, they must use the same standard. Bell 103 (300 baud) is the most common. Others include Bell 212A and Racal-Vadic (1200 baud). Some modems offer a choice of standards.

COMPUTER BULLETIN BOARD — A computer connected to the telephone lines acting as an interactive message system for any one calling in. They can be public (as most of the ones in this book) or private.

DATABASES — any collection of information stored in a computer.

DIRECT CONNECT TYPE MODEM — This type of modem plugs directly into your phone jack (if your phone has a standard modular connector). Direct connect modems are not affected by room noise.

DUPLEX — Two way communication — "Full duplex" means both sides can talk (send) and listen (receive) at the same time. We use this type of communications every day when we talk on the telephone or to each other face to face. In "half duplex" communications, each side takes turns alternately talking then listening. Most BBS's use full duplex.

ECHO — In this mode of operation (most programs are capable of this) data typed at the keyboard is echoed to the screen as well as transmitted to the remote system.

ELECTRONIC MAIL — Any private "mail" sent via telecomputing.

FILES — Computers organize input (information) and store it in related blocks called files. These files are named by the operator to be retrieved and used later.

LOGGING ON — The process of establishing contact with a remote computer system.

NETWORK — a group of people with computers in communication via telecomputing.

NULLS — The Null character is used to "be ignored and waste time". Additional nulls are especially useful when using a mechanical printer-terminal as they allow the printer to "catch up" with the transmission.

ON-LINE — to be hooked into a telecomputing network.

PARITY — Parity checking is used by the computer to make sure that each character of information is sent correctly. Parity is ODD, EVEN, or NONE. If you have any problems transferring files check to see that you have set the parity properly.

PROGRAM — (Software) A set of instructions that enables a computer to accept input (information). It then lets you tell the computer what to do with it.

PROTOCOL — A particular standard or convention for transferring data. Both systems must use the same protocol. (Christensen Protocol for RCP/M BBS, XON/XOFF, and Checksum are all common protocols used for home telecomputing.)

SYSOPS — Acronym for (SYS)tem (OP)erator — a person who runs and maintains a computer bulletin board system.

TELECOMPUTING — The transfer of information from one computer to another by any means of electronic communications usually over the (tele)phone lines.

USERS GROUPS — Computer Clubs. Can be local or national generally the BEST source of help and stimulation for the new computer user as well as the veteran. (See Resources for addresses.)

XON/XOFF — A popular protocol used in data transfer.

TROUBLESHOOTING CHART

SYMPTOM	POSSIBLE CAUSE	THINGS TO CHECK
nothing works	bad cables or connections	check all cables and connectors
	no power	make sure it is plugged in
	improper installation or operation	re-read all manuals
glitches in files transmitted/received	power line surges	install surge protection
	noisy phone lines	use error checking routines
garbage on screen or in files	mismatched baud rate or parity setting	check baud rates check parity settings
	RS-232 port mismatched	reverse pins 2 & 3
files won't transfer	wrong protocol	check protocol used by other system

INSTRUCTIONS:

After completing, remove and fold on dotted lines so that business reply address is on outside. Staple or tape closed.

For those sending check or money order, please fill out form and enclose in an envelope.

Please RUSH me the following:

☐ _____ Copies of "HOOKING IN" @ $14.95 postpaid.

☐ _____ Subscriptions to "Quarterly Update Service" @ $3.00 per Update or $10.00 per year (four issues).

Enclosed is: Cash ☐   Check ☐   Visa/MC ☐

Visa/MC # _____ Exp. Date _____

Signature _____

Make checks payable to: **ComputerFood Press, Inc.,** Div. of Coltrane & Beach

P.O. Box 6088, Oracle, AZ. 85623

☐   Please keep me posted on new ComputerFood Press Publications and Products.

Name _____

Address _____

City _____ State _____ Zip _____

☐ Please LIST the following information:

☐ New BBS   ☐ Changed Number(s)   ☐ Deleted Number(s)

System Name _____ Phone # _____

Type _____ Sysop _____

Address _____ City/St. _____

Comments _____

BUSINESS REPLY MAIL
FIRST CLASS PERMIT NO. 334 THOUSAND OAKS, CA 91360

POSTAGE WILL BE PAID BY ADDRESSEE

ComputerFood Press
DIV. OF COLTRANE & BEACH

P.O. BOX 6249
Westlake Village, CA 91359